# HE CHOSE THE NAILS

## WHAT GOD DID TO WIN YOUR HEART

BIBLE STUDY GUIDE

# MAX LUCADO

HarperChristian Resources

# CONTENTS

# A Note from Max

Have you ever wondered why God gives so much? We could exist on far less. He could have left the world flat and gray; we wouldn't have known the difference. But he didn't.

Jesus asked, "If you hard-hearted, sinful men know how to give good gifts to your children, won't your Father in heaven even more certainly give good gifts to those who ask him for them?" (Matthew 7:11 TLB). God's gifts shed light on God's heart, God's good and generous heart. Jesus' brother James tells us: "Every desirable and beneficial gift comes out of heaven. The gifts are rivers of light cascading down from the Father of Light" (James 1:17 MSG).

Every gift reveals God's love. But no gift reveals his love more than the gifts of the cross. These gifts came not wrapped in paper but in passion. Not placed around a tree but on a cross. Not covered with ribbons but sprinkled with blood.

The gifts of the cross.

Much has been said about the gift of the cross itself, but what of the other gifts? What of the nails, the crown of thorns, the garments taken by the soldiers, or the garments given for the burial? Have you taken time to open these gifts?

God didn't have to give them, you know. The only act—the only required act for our salvation—was the shedding of blood. Yet he did much more. So much more.

Search the scene of the cross, and what do you find?

A wine-soaked sponge.

A sign.

Two crosses beside Christ.

Could it be the hill of the cross is rich with God's gifts? Let's examine them. Let's unwrap these gifts of grace as if—or perhaps, indeed—for the first time. And as you touch them—as you feel the timber of the cross and trace the braid of the crown and finger the point of the spike—pause and listen. Perchance you will hear God whisper, "I did it just for you."

— MAX LUCADO

# How to Use This Guide

When some of us think of *Lent*, what comes to mind are ancient practices in the church . . . and not much else. Sure, we know what Lent is about—a forty-day season of fasting, prayer, and reflection that leads into Easter Sunday—but it's not something we do in our church. While we like the idea of focusing more on Jesus in the weeks leading up to Easter, and are even curious about what it would look like to engage with Christians around the world who celebrate Lent, we're not sure where to start or what commitment it would take. And we're also not sure about all the talk we've heard of "giving up" something for Lent.

Well, if you've ever felt this way, you've come to the right place! The *He Chose the Nails Bible Study* will give you a simple framework for how to spend time with God and dwell in his Word for each of the forty days leading into Easter. And when it comes to giving up something for Lent . . . you are going to look at that from a different perspective. Instead of thinking about what *you* will give up, you will look at what *Jesus* gave up for you. Specifically, you will look at the "gifts" that Jesus gave to you at the cross.

Before you begin, there are a few ways you can go through this material. You can experience this study in a group (such as a Bible study, Sunday school class, or other small group gathering), or you can go through the content on your own. Either way, the videos are available to view at any time by following the instructions provided with this study guide.

## GROUP STUDY

Each of the sessions in this study guide are divided into two parts: (1) a group study section and (2) a personal study section. The group study section provides a basic framework on how to open your time together, get the most out of the video content, and discuss the key ideas that were presented in the teaching. Each session includes the following:

- **Welcome:** A short opening note about the topic of the session for you to read on your own before you meet as a group.

- **Connect:** A few icebreaker questions to get you and your group members thinking about the topic and interacting with each other.

- **Watch:** An outline of the key points covered in each video teaching along with space for you to take notes as you watch each session.

- **Discuss:** Questions to help you and your group reflect on the teaching material presented and apply it to your lives.

- **Respond:** A closing exercise for you to do with your group.

- **Pray:** A reminder to reflect on prayer requests and praises for the week.

If you are doing this study in a group, make sure you have your own copy of the study guide so you can write down your thoughts, responses, and reflections in the space provided—and so you have access to the videos via streaming. You will also want to have a copy of the *He Chose the Nails* book, as reading it alongside this guide will provide you with deeper insights. (See the notes at the beginning of each group session and personal study section on which chapters of the book you should read before the next group session.)

Finally, keep these points in mind:

- **Facilitation:** If you are doing this study in a group, you will want to appoint someone to serve as a facilitator. This person will be responsible for starting the video and keeping track of time during discussions and activities.

- **Faithfulness:** Your group is a place where tremendous growth can happen as you reflect on the Bible, ask questions, and learn what God is doing in other people's lives. For this reason, be fully committed and attend each session so you can build trust and rapport with the other members.

- **Friendship:** The goal of any small group is to serve as a place where people can share, learn about God, and build friendships. So make your group a safe place. Be honest about your thoughts and feelings, but also listen carefully to everyone else's thoughts, feelings, and opinions. Keep anything personal that your group members share in confidence so that you can create a community where people can heal, be challenged, and grow spiritually.

If you are going through this study on your own, read the opening Welcome section and reflect on the questions in the Connect section. Watch the video and use the outline provided to help you take notes. Finally, personalize the questions and exercises in the Discuss and Respond sections. Close by recording any requests you want to pray about during the week.

Note that *He Chose the Nails* includes five teaching videos from Max that correspond to sessions 1 to 5 in this study guide (which will take you through Day 35 of Lent). An additional non-video session has been provided if you and your group want to meet together for the full forty days of Lent.[1] This bonus session does not include a video outline or space for taking notes but features additional questions for an extended group discussion time.

## LENTEN PRACTICES

The forty daily Lenten practices in this study guide will give you the opportunity to connect with God throughout each week and prepare your heart for Easter. These practices encourage you to set aside a brief amount of time each day—in the morning and evening—to slow down, reflect, and just talk with your heavenly Father. Most of the readings are from *The Daily Office*, a set of daily prayer liturgies from the *Book of Common Prayer*.[2] To get the most out of these practices, try not rush them or leave them until the last minute to complete.

Further instructions on how to complete the daily Lenten practices are provided after each group section in this guide. However, if you're participating in this study with a group, it's important to remember that your *presence* matters more than your *progress*. Even if you haven't completed the exercises for the week, or haven't started at all, you are still a welcome part of the group. The material in this study guide is simply intended to be a resource to help you *hear* what God wants you to hear, *apply* what he is saying to your life, and develop some practical prayer and study *habits* around the Lenten/Easter season.

| | |
|---|---|
| **BEFORE GROUP MEETING** | Read the introduction and chapters 1–3 in *He Chose the Nails* <br> Read the Welcome section (page 2) |
| **GROUP MEETING** | Discuss the Connect questions <br> Watch the video teaching for session 1 <br> Discuss the questions that follow as a group <br> Do the closing exercise and pray (pages 2–8) |
| **LENTEN PRACTICES:** <br> DAYS 1 TO 7 | Complete the daily Lenten Practices (pages 9–20) |
| **CATCH UP AND READ AHEAD** <br> (BEFORE WEEK 2 GROUP MEETING) | Complete the Week in Review (page 21) <br> Read chapters 4–7 in *He Chose the Nails* |

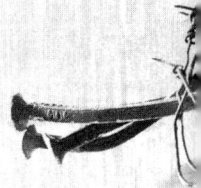

# HE CHOSE TO BE ONE OF US

*God did what the law could not do. He sent his own Son in a body like the bodies we sinners have. And in that body God declared an end to sin's control over us by giving his Son as a sacrifice for our sins.*

ROMANS 8:3 NLT

*You alone are the God for us—because you alone are the God who has been one of us. You felt what we feel, you touched the death that we know, you came to us as Immanuel: God with us.*

ANN VOSKAMP, *A HOLY EXPERIENCE*[3]

## WELCOME [READ ON YOUR OWN]

Today, most of the products in our world are mass-produced by machines churning out thousands of identical pairs of T-shirts, coffee mugs, and automobiles. Yet there was a time, many years ago, when everything was handmade. Homes were built using bricks formed of clay and straw. Vessels used for drinking, cooking, and storage were constructed from pottery. Stone tools were crafted for hunting. Men and women dedicated years to their craft, perfecting their techniques, skills, and artistry until they were called master craftsmen or artisans.

In the first-century Roman world, skilled craftsmen also created crowns by hand. Some of these—especially those used in official ceremonies—were made of gold bands adorned with precious stones and required techniques such as metalwork, engraving, and gemstone setting. Other crowns were simpler. Roman soldiers who saved a comrade in battle were awarded a crown made of oak leaves. Soldiers who saved an entire army from siege (the highest military honor) were given a crown made of grass, weeds, and wildflowers from the battlefield. Partygoers at Roman festivals wore crowns made of myrtle, violets, ivy, or parsley.

One material *not* used in making crowns was thornbushes. Yet this is exactly what the Roman soldiers "twisted together" for Jesus and set on his head (Matthew 27:29). Far from conveying what the typical Roman crown was meant to symbolize—victory, praise, honor, divinity, and celebration—this crown of thorns was meant to symbolize Jesus' public shame and mockery of his claim to kingship. Yet little did these soldiers know that what they designed as a symbol of humiliation would prove to be one of the greatest gifts of the cross. For Jesus bore *our* sin and humiliation willingly, taking on himself the punishment that we deserved.

## CONNECT [15 MINUTES]

If you or any of your group members don't know each other, take a few minutes to introduce yourselves. Then discuss one or both of the following questions.

- How would you describe your understanding and experience of Lent over the years?

— or —

- What, if anything, shifts in your perspective when you think of Lent less as a season of guilt or giving something up and more as a time to be intentional about preparing to receive joy and good things from God?

## WATCH [20 MINUTES]

Watch the video for this session, which you can access through streaming (see the instructions provided with this guide). Below is an outline of the key points covered during the teaching.

### OUTLINE

I. **God's boundless love**
   A. God's greatest gift of all—his greatest act of love for us—was sending Jesus into our world.
   B. Think how amazing this gift was and what God gave up to make it happen:
      1. **Timelessness:** Jesus swapped eternity for calendars. As the Savior, he left behind the boundless nature of heaven where there was no such thing as "your time is up."
      2. **Boundlessness:** Jesus gave up being a spirit to live in a body. One moment he was a boundless spirit; the next he was flesh and bones.
      3. **Sinlessness:** Jesus became sin for us. An object that symbolizes the consequences of sin in humanity's heart is a thornbush.

II. **Rebellion results in thorns**
   A. In the Bible, an object that symbolizes the consequences of sin in humanity's heart is a thornbush.
   B. If the fruit of sin is thorns, isn't the thorny crown on Christ's brow a picture of the fruit of our sin that pierced his heart?
      1. What is the fruit of sin? *Shame. Fear. Disgrace. Discouragement. Anxiety.*
      2. The heart of Jesus had never been cut by the thorns of sin. As John tells us, "God is light; in him there is no darkness at all" (1 John 1:5).
      3. Jesus never knew the fruits of sin until he became sin for us (see 2 Corinthians 5:21).

III. **Corrupt at the core**
   A. Paul tells us we are "by nature children of wrath" (Ephesians 2:3 NASB).
   B. Though we have been made in God's image, we're corrupt. In theological terms, we are "totally depraved."
   C. The sinless One took on the face of a sinner so that we sinners could take on the face of a saint.
   D. When Jesus was crucified, he cried out in a loud voice, "My God, my God, why have you forsaken me?" (Matthew 27:46). Those are not the words of a saint but the cry of a sinner.

## IV. His great love

A. The crown of thorns could have been made—and should have been worn— by every one of us.

B. Jesus bore our sin willingly, taking the punishment we deserved.

C. Why did God give us this gift? "For God so loved the world that he gave his one and only Son, that whoever believes in him shall not perish but have eternal life" (John 3:16).

D. God did it for us—just for us—because he loves us.

## NOTES

_____
_____
_____
_____
_____
_____
_____
_____
_____
_____
_____
_____
_____
_____
_____
_____
_____
_____
_____
_____
_____
_____
_____
_____
_____
_____
_____
_____
_____

## DISCUSS [35 MINUTES]

Discuss what you just watched by answering the following questions.

1. Consider the typical response you have when you receive a gift. Do you send any "thought zingers," such as *I don't deserve this; I had better not waste this; someone else needs this more.* What other internal dynamics make it difficult for you to truly receive a gift?

2. The sense of Lent is evident in the words of Jesus: "The kingdom of God has come near. Repent and believe the good news!" (Mark 1:15). We also find it in this passage written by the prophet Joel, traditionally read at the beginning of Lent:

   "Even now," declares the Lord, "return to me with all your heart, with fasting and weeping and mourning." Rend your heart and not your garments. Return to the Lord your God, for he is gracious and compassionate, slow to anger and abounding in love, and he relents from sending calamity (Joel 2:12–13).

   The Hebrew verbs translated *rend* and *return* in this passage are images of repentance in action. People would rend or tear their garments as an expression of intense grief.[4] To return means to make a U-turn, to go back to the point of departure, to change one's mind.[5] What do these two words—*rend* and *return*—suggest about what it means not only to seek reconciliation with God but also to do so with all your heart?

3. Drawing on any previous experiences of repentance and forgiveness (with God or others), what three words or phrases would you use to describe what it's like to *rend* your heart?

4. The crown of thorns the Roman soldiers made for Jesus was intended to not only be a means of physical torture but also of humiliation. However, in making it a gift of the cross, God utterly transformed it. Consider this particular gift of the cross—of allowing God to transform whatever has been a source of pain and shame into a crown of victory and glory. What might make it difficult to truly receive this gift? What would receiving this gift require of a person throughout his or her walk with God?

5. As you anticipate learning more about the gifts of Easter, how does this perspective about receiving God's gifts challenge you? In what ways does it intrigue or encourage you?

## RESPOND [10 MINUTES]

In addition to studying together, it's also important to walk together through Lent—to share your lives with one another and be aware of how God is at work among you. In each session, there will be opportunities to speak life-giving words and to listen to one another deeply. Use one or two of the sentence starters below, or your own statement, to help the group understand the best way to be a good friend to you throughout this study. As each person responds, use the chart that follows to briefly note what is important to that person and how you can be a good friend to him or her during your discussions and times together.

- *You can help me to take Lent seriously this year by . . .*
- *I'd like you to consistently challenge me about . . .*
- *It really helps me to engage in a group when . . .*
- *I tend to withdraw or feel anxious when . . .*
- *In our discussions, the best thing you could do for me is . . .*

| Name | The best way I can be a good friend to this person is . . . |
|------|------------------------------------------------------------|
|      |                                                            |
|      |                                                            |
|      |                                                            |

| Name | The best way I can be a good friend to this person is . . . |
|------|------------------------------------------------------------|
|      |                                                            |
|      |                                                            |
|      |                                                            |
|      |                                                            |
|      |                                                            |

## PRAY [10 MINUTES]

Take a moment to give thanks for the gift of the crown of thorns. Ask God to remove any distractions that take your gaze away from Jesus' sacrifice. Record any prayer requests or praises so you and your group members can pray about them in the week ahead.

# LENTEN PRACTICE

*Let's take a good look at the way we're living
and reorder our lives under GOD.*

LAMENTATIONS 3:40 MSG

The starting point for Lent requires holding two things in tension: a humble reckoning of our sinful condition and an expectation we will be changed. It is a spring-cleaning of the soul that gives us permission to take seriously the areas of our lives in which we fall short, feel defeated, or have grown cold. And it is a kindling of the soul that sparks our desire to return to God with our whole heart. The author of Hebrews captures this demanding yet joyful spirit of Lent:

> Let us strip off every weight that slows us down, especially the sin that so easily trips us up. And let us run with endurance the race God has set before us. We do this by keeping our eyes on Jesus, the champion who initiates and perfects our faith. Because of the joy awaiting him, he endured the cross, disregarding its shame (12:1–2 NLT).

The Lenten journey, in preparation for Easter, requires us to commit to an honest examination of our lives but not morbid introspection. We let go of hindrances but not our status as children of God. In all things, we do not lose sight of where we're headed—an exhilarating new life with Christ! We keep our eyes fixed on Jesus and the joy before us.

The practice for this week—which you will build on throughout this study—is to set aside time each day to listen to God through Scripture and prayerful reflection. The invitation is to cultivate a humble spirit of hope and expectation that God will meet you in this practice if you are willing to trust him. Author and pastor N. T. Wright writes:

> Whenever God does something new, he involves people—often unlikely people, frequently surprised and alarmed people. He asks them to trust him in a new way, to put aside their natural reactions, to listen humbly

9

for a fresh word and to act on it without knowing exactly how it's going to work out. That's what he's asking all of us to do this Lent. Reading the Bible without knowing in advance what God is going to say takes humility. . . . We may have to put our initial reactions on hold and be prepared to hear new words, to think new thoughts, and to live them out.[6]

Each day this week, the goal is to set aside a few minutes to read, prayerfully reflect on the daily Scripture readings, and spend time with God. The readings include morning and evening psalms as well as selections from the Old Testament, New Testament epistles, and the Gospels.

Here is a general overview of what each day will look like:

- Begin in the morning with a brief time of silence (one to two minutes). Then, in God's presence, reflect on these questions:

  ▸ *Where am I falling short, feeling defeated, or growing cold to God?*
  ▸ *What new thing do I want God to do in my life?*

- Next, ask the Lord to speak to you through what you are about to read. Go over the Scripture passages for the morning slowly and prayerfully, paying attention to any words, phrases, or verses that stand out to you. You're looking for what is sometimes referred to as **watchwords**—anything that sparks a connection between the text and your life. It might be a promise, a word of wisdom, an admonition, a comfort, or an encouragement.

- Read your morning watchwords again, receiving what you read as God's words especially for you. Then reflect on the following questions:

  ▸ *What do I sense God is saying to me?*
  ▸ *If I took these words seriously, how would I respond?*

- Sometime later in the day, read the evening psalm slowly and prayerfully, again paying attention to any words, phrases, or verses that stand out to you. Write down your evening **watchwords** for this psalm.

- Read these watchwords again, and then reflect on the following questions:

  ▸ *What do I sense God is saying to me?*
  ▸ *If I took these words seriously, how would I respond?*

- Close by asking God to help you to "hear new words, to think new thoughts, and to live them out." Invite God to use your watchwords to continue speaking to you throughout the rest of the day. Write down any other observations about your experience of reading God's Word and listening for his voice.

- At the end of the week, review your daily reflections and observations. What stands out most to you about what God is saying to you? Write your observations in the space provided or in your journal.

Bring your notes to the next group gathering if you are doing the study with others, as you will have a chance to talk about your observations at the beginning of the session.

# DAY 1

## PREPARATION

Begin each day with a time of silence (one to two minutes). Be still for just a few moments to free your mind from distractions and worries so you can focus on your time with the Lord.

## REFLECTION

*Lord, where am I falling short, feeling defeated, or growing cold to you? What new thing do I want you to do in my life?*

## MORNING READING

Remember each day to ask the Lord to speak to you through what you are about to read. Pay attention to any words, phrases, or verses that stand out to you.

- **Psalm:** Psalms 63; 95
- **Epistle:** Hebrews 2:10–18
- **Old Testament:** Daniel 9:3–10
- **Gospel:** John 12:44–50

**Watchwords** (anything that sparks a connection between the text and your life):

*What do I sense God is saying to me? If I took these words seriously, how would I respond?*

## EVENING READING

Once again, ask the Lord to speak to you through what you are about to read.

> • **Psalm:** Psalm 103

**Watchwords:**

*What do I sense God is saying to me? If I took these words seriously, how would I respond?*

## CLOSE

Close each day by asking God to help you *hear new words, think new thoughts, and live them out.* Invite the Lord to use your watchwords to continue speaking to you throughout the rest of the day. Journal any other observations about your experience.

# DAY 2

## REFLECTION

*Lord, where am I falling short, feeling defeated, or growing cold to you? What new thing do I want you to do in my life?*

## MORNING READING

- **Psalm:** Psalms 41; 52
- **Epistle:** 1 Corinthians 1:1–19
- **Old Testament:** Genesis 37:1–11
- **Gospel:** Mark 1:1–39

**Watchwords:**

*What do I sense God is saying to me? If I took these words seriously, how would I respond?*

## EVENING READING

- **Psalm:** Psalm 44

**Watchwords:**

*What do I sense God is saying to me? If I took these words seriously, how would I respond?*

# DAY 3

## REFLECTION

*Lord, where am I falling short, feeling defeated, or growing cold to you? What new thing do I want you to do in my life?*

## MORNING READING

- **Psalm:** Psalm 45
- **Epistle:** 1 Corinthians 1:20–31
- **Old Testament:** Genesis 37:12–24
- **Gospel:** Mark 1:40–2:12

**Watchwords:**

*What do I sense God is saying to me? If I took these words seriously, how would I respond?*

## EVENING READING

- **Psalm:** Psalms 47; 48

**Watchwords:**

*What do I sense God is saying to me? If I took these words seriously, how would I respond?*

# DAY 4

## REFLECTION

*Lord, where am I falling short, feeling defeated, or growing cold to you? What new thing do I want you to do in my life?*

## MORNING READING

- **Psalm:** Psalm 119:49–72
- **Epistle:** 1 Corinthians 2:1–13
- **Old Testament:** Genesis 37:25–36
- **Gospel:** Mark 2:13–28

**Watchwords:**

*What do I sense God is saying to me? If I took these words seriously, how would I respond?*

## EVENING READING

- **Psalm:** Psalms 49; 53

**Watchwords:**

*What do I sense God is saying to me? If I took these words seriously, how would I respond?*

# DAY 5

## REFLECTION

*Lord, where am I falling short, feeling defeated, or growing cold to you? What new thing do I want you to do in my life?*

## MORNING READING

- **Psalm:** Psalm 50
- **Epistle:** 1 Corinthians 2:14–3:15
- **Old Testament:** Genesis 39:1–23
- **Gospel:** Mark 3:1–19

**Watchwords:**

*What do I sense God is saying to me? If I took these words seriously, how would I respond?*

## EVENING READING

- **Psalm:** Psalms 59; 60

**Watchwords:**

*What do I sense God is saying to me? If I took these words seriously, how would I respond?*

# Day 6

## REFLECTION

*Lord, where am I falling short, feeling defeated, or growing cold to you? What new thing do I want you to do in my life?*

## MORNING READING

- **Psalm:** Psalms 40; 54
- **Epistle:** 1 Corinthians 3:16–23
- **Old Testament:** Genesis 40:1–23
- **Gospel:** Mark 3:20–35

**Watchwords:**

*What do I sense God is saying to me? If I took these words seriously, how would I respond?*

## EVENING READING

- **Psalm:** Psalm 51

**Watchwords:**

*What do I sense God is saying to me? If I took these words seriously, how would I respond?*

# DAY 7

## REFLECTION

*Lord, where am I falling short, feeling defeated, or growing cold to you? What new thing do I want you to do in my life?*

## MORNING READING

- **Psalm:** Psalm 55
- **Epistle:** 1 Corinthians 4:1–7
- **Old Testament:** Genesis 41:1–13
- **Gospel:** Mark 4:1–20

**Watchwords:**

*What do I sense God is saying to me? If I took these words seriously, how would I respond?*

## EVENING READING

- **Psalm:** Psalms 138; 139

**Watchwords:**

*What do I sense God is saying to me? If I took these words seriously, how would I respond?*

# WEEK IN REVIEW

Review the daily reflections and observations that you recorded during the course of this week. *What stands out most to you about what God is saying to you?*

Read chapters 4–7 in *He Chose the Nails* before the next group gathering. Use the space below to make note of anything that stands out to you or encourages you.

| | |
|---|---|
| **BEFORE GROUP MEETING** | Read chapters 4–7 in *He Chose the Nails* Read the Welcome section (page 24) |
| **GROUP MEETING** | Discuss the Connect questions Watch the video teaching for session 2 Discuss the questions that follow as a group Do the closing exercise and pray (pages 24–30) |
| **LENTEN PRACTICES:** DAYS 8 TO 14 | Complete the daily Lenten practices (pages 31–42) |
| **CATCH UP AND READ AHEAD** (BEFORE WEEK 3 GROUP MEETING) | Complete the Week in Review (page 43) Read chapters 8–10 in *He Chose the Nails* |

# HE CHOSE TO FORGIVE US

*When you were stuck in your old sin-dead life, you were incapable of responding to God. God brought you alive—right along with Christ! Think of it! All sins forgiven, the slate wiped clean, that old arrest warrant canceled and nailed to Christ's cross.*

COLOSSIANS 2:13-14 MSG

*No sin is written with indelible ink.*

ALBERT HAASE,
*LIVING THE LORD'S PRAYER*[7]

## WELCOME [READ ON YOUR OWN]

Picture the scene. The silhouette of a figure stands in front of a blazing forge. He uses tongs to pull out a glowing piece of metal and places it on an anvil.

He picks up a hammer and strikes the metal once . . . twice . . . then again and again . . . purposefully shaping the metal to fit the image in his mind. Suddenly, he picks up the metal and dunks it into a pail of water. A cloud of steam rises. The blacksmith fishes out the finished piece—a nail—and drops it into a bin.

The earliest nails, based on archaeological finds from ancient Egyptian sites, date to around 3300 BC. These nails were made of bronze and appear to have been primarily used in shipbuilding (for boats on the Nile) and furniture making. As the centuries passed and methods of working metal improved, bronze nails were replaced by nails made of iron, which were more versatile and durable. The Romans were the first to mass-produce iron nails, using them in ships, fortifications, and even in scaffolding used to construct aqueducts.[8]

Many people saw these acts of Roman engineering as gifts to the world. Ships united people groups and increased trade. Fortifications protected populations. Aqueducts carried fresh water to cities. But few would have said the same of another purpose the Roman nails served: attaching a convicted criminal's wrists and feet to a wooden cross. While the Persians invented crucifixion, the Romans perfected it into a slow and painful means of execution. It was an excruciating way to die. Yet the nails used in Jesus' crucifixion were indeed a gift, for God would use them to accomplish his plans for humanity.

## CONNECT [15 MINUTES]

A key part of getting to know God better is sharing your journey with others. Before watching the video, take a moment to discuss with one another your experiences since the last session. Then discuss one or both of the following questions:

- Briefly share your experience of the Lenten practice you did last week. The focus of this practice was to set aside time each day to listen to God. How did you do? Did you find it difficult or relatively easy? Why?

— or —

- What was it like to read and reflect on the daily scriptures, knowing everyone else in the group was reading the same passages that day? In what ways, if any, did you find it meaningful or different than reading on your own?

# WATCH [20 MINUTES]

Now watch the video for this session. Below is an outline of the key points covered during the teaching. Record any key concepts that stand out to you.

## OUTLINE

**I.  The gift of the nails**

  A.  Nails fix broken things. They join together things that were separated. They make things whole.

  B.  God used nails to accomplish his plan. The nails in that cross show us the lengths God will go to cover our sins and restore our relationship with him.

**II. The road to the cross**

  A.  The most notorious road in the world is the Via Dolorosa, the "Way of Sorrows." According to tradition, it is the route Jesus took from Pilate's hall to Calvary.

  B.  Yet the path began not in the court of Pilate but in the halls of heaven. The Father began his journey when he left his home in search of us.

  C.  Armed with nothing more than a passion to win our hearts, he came looking. His desire was singular—to bring his children home. The Bible has a word for this quest: *reconciliation*.

**III. Reconciliation with God**

  A.  The apostle Paul tells us, "God was in Christ reconciling the world to Himself" (2 Corinthians 5:19 NKJV). The Greek word for *reconcile* means "to render something otherwise."

  B.  Reconciliation restitches the unraveled, reverses the rebellion, and rekindles the cold passion. It touches the shoulder of the wayward and woos him homeward.

  C.  Paul speaks bluntly of our condition in Romans 5:10: "We were God's enemies." Yet even in spite of our actions, Paul tells us "we were reconciled to him through the death of his Son."

**IV. The hands of Jesus**

  A.  Between Jesus' hand and the wood is a list of our mistakes: our lusts, and lies, and greedy moments, and prodigal years.

  B.  Since Jesus couldn't bear the thought of eternity without us—and in spite of the fact that we were his enemies—he chose the nails.

C. He knew that the purpose of the nail was to place our sins where they could be hidden by his sacrifice and covered by his blood.

D. Your sins have been blotted out by Jesus. "Christ has utterly wiped out the damning evidence of broken laws and commandments which always hung over our heads, and has completely annulled it by nailing it over his own head on the cross" (Colossians 2:14 PHILLIPS).

## NOTES

## DISCUSS [35 MINUTES]

Discuss what you just watched by answering the following questions.

1. In Colossians 1:21–23, Paul describes our condition prior to reconciliation as that of "enemies." The Greek word Paul uses is *echthros*, a derivative of the Greek word for *hatred*. So, the literal translation of *echthros* would be "haters." It conveys the idea of "irreconcilable, deep-rooted enmity . . . someone from whom one can expect only harm and danger."[9] To better understand what this enemy condition really means, use the space below to list whoever comes to mind in connection with the phrases "enemies of God" or "God haters." After one minute, go around the group and read what you wrote, but with one addition: Add your *own name* as the last item on your list.

2. What is it like to hear your own name included on a list of God's enemies and to know that it's true—that it accurately describes your condition before you gave your life to Christ? In what ways, if any, are you tempted to resist, minimize, or otherwise rationalize this truth about yourself? What makes it hard to accept that it really is true?

3. Reconciliation is God's gift to his enemies.[10] In Colossians 1:21–23, the Greek word Paul uses for *reconciliation* is *apokatallassō*—the root word of which means to alter or exchange. In reconciliation, God offers his enemies friendship in exchange for hatred. It makes sense that we might distance ourselves from the truth of our enemy status with God, but why might we also distance ourselves from the truth of our reconciliation?

4. It wasn't an angry mob, jealous religious leaders, or even Roman soldiers who crucified Jesus. It was *Jesus himself* who chose the nails. Why is it so critical to understand this—that Jesus was not a victim but made a sacrificial choice from a position of authority?

5. Part of the invitation of Lent is to take seriously things we might otherwise gloss over—not only the gravity of sin and our need for forgiveness but also the depth of Christ's love and the magnitude of his sacrifice for us. What hopes or fears come to mind when you consider taking Christ's love for you more seriously than you do right now?

## RESPOND [10 MINUTES]

In the last session, you were given the opportunity to provide feedback on how your group members can be a good friend to you during this study and how you can be a good friend to them. Take a moment to add any group members who were absent from the last session and make any clarifications the group might have. Here again are the conversation starters:

- *You can help me to take Lent seriously this year by . . .*
- *I'd like you to consistently challenge me about . . .*
- *It really helps me to engage in a group when . . .*
- *I tend to withdraw or feel anxious when . . .*
- *In our discussions, the best thing you could do for me is . . .*

| Name | The best way I can be a good friend to this person is . . . |
|------|-----------------------------------------------------------|
|      |                                                           |
|      |                                                           |
|      |                                                           |
|      |                                                           |

| Name | The best way I can be a good friend to this person is . . . |
|------|---------------------------------------------------------------|
|      |                                                               |
|      |                                                               |
|      |                                                               |
|      |                                                               |
|      |                                                               |

## PRAY [10 MINUTES]

Take a moment to give thanks for the gift of the nails. Ask God to remove any distractions that take your gaze away from Jesus' sacrifice. Record any prayer requests or praises so you and your group members can pray about them in the week ahead.

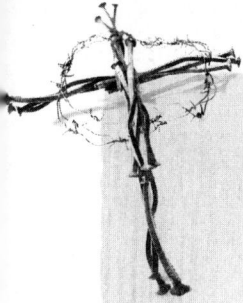

# LENTEN PRACTICE

*Seek GOD while he's here to be found, pray to him while
he's close at hand. . . . Come back to GOD, who is merciful,
come back to our God, who is lavish with forgiveness.*

ISAIAH 55:6–7 MSG

The promise of reconciliation is peace with God (see Colossians 1:19–20). And
yet, as much as we want peace with God, we also might find ourselves shrinking
back from it. Reconciliation requires coming to grips with sin we often prefer
to minimize, overlook, or avoid. The key is to allow our sin to lead us into an
even deeper immersion in the wonder of God's love and acceptance. Author
and pastor Timothy Keller writes:

> The gospel of justifying faith means that while Christians are, in
> themselves still sinful and sinning, yet in Christ, in God's sight, they
> are accepted and righteous. So we can say that we are more wicked
> than we ever dared believe, but more loved and accepted in Christ
> than we ever dared hope—at the very same time. This creates a radi-
> cal new dynamic for personal growth. It means that the more you see
> your own flaws and sins, the more precious, electrifying, and amazing
> God's grace appears to you. But on the other hand, the more aware
> you are of God's grace and acceptance in Christ, the more able you
> are to drop your denials and self-defenses and admit the true dimen-
> sions and character of your sin.[11]

This week, you will take another step in preparing your heart for Easter
by seeking to make God's grace "more precious, electrifying, and amazing"
through confession and by continuing to set aside time each day to listen to
God through Scripture.

Here again is a general overview of what each day will look like this week:

- Begin in the morning with a brief time of silence (one to two minutes). Then, in God's presence, reflect on these questions:

  ▸ *Where do I lack peace with God?*
  ▸ *For what do I need God's forgiveness?*

- Consider one-time failures as well as any ongoing habits of thought or behavior that come between you and God. If you find it helpful, refer back to your written reflections from last week in response to the question: *Where am I falling short, feeling defeated, or growing cold to God?*

- Next, with specificity, confess to God the wrong you have done or the good you have left undone. Express your regret and sorrow, asking him to forgive you and to give you "the desire and the power to do what pleases him" (Philippians 2:13 NLT). Receive God's forgiveness, expressing your wonder at the tenderness of his grace and thanking him for his peace.

- Ask the Lord to speak to you through what you are about to read. Go over Scripture passages for the morning slowly and prayerfully, paying attention to anything that sparks a connection between the text and your life. These are your morning **watchwords**. Again, these could be a promise, a word of wisdom, an admonition, a comfort, or an encouragement.

- Read your morning watchwords again, receiving what you read as God's words especially for you. Then reflect on the following questions:

  ▸ *What do I sense God is saying to me?*
  ▸ *If I took these words seriously, how would I respond?*

- Sometime later in the day, read the evening psalm slowly and prayerfully, again paying attention to any words, phrases, or verses that stand out to you. Write down your evening **watchwords** for this psalm.

- Read these watchwords again, and then reflect on the following questions:

  ▸ *What do I sense God is saying to me?*
  ▸ *If I took these words seriously, how would I respond?*

- Close by asking God to help you live in the assurance of his forgiveness and peace. Invite him to use your watchwords to continue speaking to you throughout the rest of the day. Write down any other observations about your experience of reading God's Word and listening for his voice.

- At the end of the week, review your daily reflections and observations. What stands out most to you about what God is saying to you? Write your observations in the space provided or in your journal.

Bring your notes to the next group gathering if you are doing the study with others, as you will have a chance to talk about your observations at the beginning of the session.

# DAY 8

## PREPARATION

Begin each day with a time of silence (one to two minutes). Be still for just a few moments to free your mind from distractions and worries so you can focus on your time with the Lord.

## REFLECTION

*Lord, where do I lack peace with you? For what do I need your forgiveness?*

## MORNING READING

Remember each day to confess to God the wrong you have done or the good you have left undone. Ask him to speak to you through what you are about to read. Pay attention to any words, phrases, or verses that stand out to you.

- **Psalm:** Psalms 24; 95
- **Epistle:** Romans 6:3–14
- **Old Testament:** Genesis 41:14–45
- **Gospel:** John 5:19–24

**Watchwords** (anything that sparks a connection between the text and your life):

*What do I sense God is saying to me? If I took these words seriously, how would I respond?*

## EVENING READING

Once again, ask the Lord to speak to you through what you are about to read.

> • **Psalm:** Psalms 8; 84

**Watchwords:**

*What do I sense God is saying to me? If I took these words seriously, how would I respond?*

## CLOSE

Close each day by asking God to help you live in the assurance of his forgiveness and peace. Invite him to use your watchwords to continue speaking to you throughout the rest of the day. Journal any other observations about your experience.

# DAY 9

## REFLECTION

*Lord, where do I lack peace with you? For what do I need your forgiveness?*

## MORNING READING

- **Psalm:** Psalms 56; 57; 58
- **Epistle:** 1 Corinthians 4:8–21
- **Old Testament:** Genesis 41:46–57
- **Gospel:** Mark 4:21–5:20

**Watchwords:**

*What do I sense God is saying to me? If I took these words seriously, how would I respond?*

## EVENING READING

- **Psalm:** Psalms 64; 65

**Watchwords:**

*What do I sense God is saying to me? If I took these words seriously, how would I respond?*

# DAY 10

## REFLECTION

*Lord, where do I lack peace with you? For what do I need your forgiveness?*

## MORNING READING

- **Psalm:** Psalms 61; 62
- **Epistle:** 1 Corinthians 5:1–8
- **Old Testament:** Genesis 42:1–17
- **Gospel:** Mark 5:21–34

Watchwords:

*What do I sense God is saying to me? If I took these words seriously, how would I respond?*

## EVENING READING

- **Psalm:** Psalm 68

Watchwords:

*What do I sense God is saying to me? If I took these words seriously, how would I respond?*

# DAY 11

## REFLECTION

*Lord, where do I lack peace with you? For what do I need your forgiveness?*

## MORNING READING

- **Psalm:** Psalm 72
- **Epistle:** 1 Corinthians 5:9–6:8
- **Old Testament:** Genesis 42:18–28
- **Gospel:** Mark 5:35–6:6

**Watchwords:**

*What do I sense God is saying to me? If I took these words seriously, how would I respond?*

## EVENING READING

- **Psalm:** Psalm 119:73–96

**Watchwords:**

*What do I sense God is saying to me? If I took these words seriously, how would I respond?*

# DAY 12

## REFLECTION

*Lord, where do I lack peace with you? For what do I need your forgiveness?*

## MORNING READING

- **Psalm:** Psalms 70; 71
- **Epistle:** 1 Corinthians 6:9–20
- **Old Testament:** Genesis 42:29–38
- **Gospel:** Mark 6:7–29

**Watchwords:**

*What do I sense God is saying to me? If I took these words seriously, how would I respond?*

## EVENING READING

- **Psalm:** Psalm 74

**Watchwords:**

*What do I sense God is saying to me? If I took these words seriously, how would I respond?*

# DAY 13

## REFLECTION

*Lord, where do I lack peace with you? For what do I need your forgiveness?*

## MORNING READING

- **Psalm:** Psalm 69
- **Epistle:** 1 Corinthians 7:1–9
- **Old Testament:** Genesis 43:1–15
- **Gospel:** Mark 6:30–44

**Watchwords:**

*What do I sense God is saying to me? If I took these words seriously, how would I respond?*

## EVENING READING

- **Psalm:** Psalm 73

**Watchwords:**

*What do I sense God is saying to me? If I took these words seriously, how would I respond?*

# DAY 14

## REFLECTION

*Lord, where do I lack peace with you? For what do I need your forgiveness?*

## MORNING READING

- **Psalm:** Psalms 75; 76
- **Epistle:** 1 Corinthians 7:10-24
- **Old Testament:** Genesis 43:16-34
- **Gospel:** Mark 6:45-56

**Watchwords:**

*What do I sense God is saying to me? If I took these words seriously, how would I respond?*

## EVENING READING

- **Psalm:** Psalms 23; 27

**Watchwords:**

*What do I sense God is saying to me? If I took these words seriously, how would I respond?*

# WEEK IN REVIEW

Review the daily reflections and observations that you recorded during the course of this week. *What stands out most to you about what God is saying to you?*

Read chapters 8–10 in *He Chose the Nails* before the next group gathering. Use the space below to make note of anything that stands out to you or encourages you.

| | |
|---|---|
| **BEFORE GROUP MEETING** | Read chapters 8–10 in *He Chose the Nails* Read the Welcome section (page 46) |
| **GROUP MEETING** | Discuss the Connect questions Watch the video teaching for session 3 Discuss the questions that follow as a group Do the closing exercise and pray (pages 46–50) |
| **LENTEN PRACTICES:** DAYS 15 TO 21 | Complete the daily Lenten practices (pages 51–62) |
| **CATCH UP AND READ AHEAD** (BEFORE WEEK 4 GROUP MEETING) | Complete the Week in Review (page 63) Read chapters 11–13 in *He Chose the Nails* |

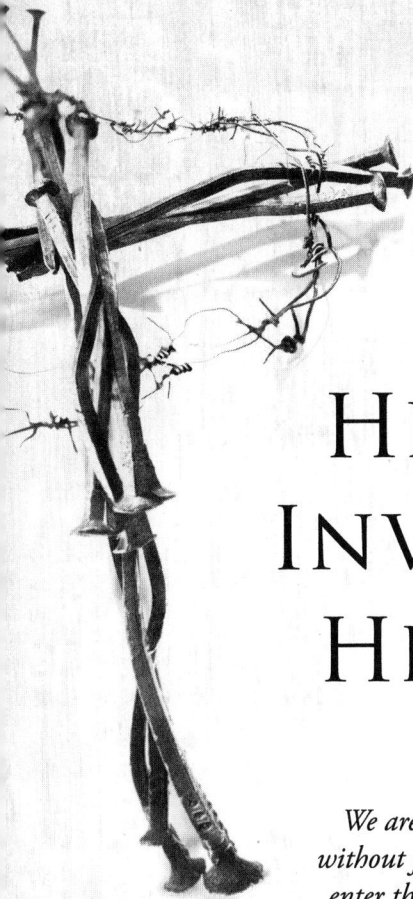

# He Chose to Invite Us into His Presence

*We are completely free to enter the Most Holy Place without fear because of the blood of Jesus' death. We can enter through a new and living way that Jesus opened for us. It leads through the curtain—Christ's body.*

HEBREWS 10:19-20 NCV

*Christ has gone into the glory of the Father, and he has made a way for us to enter into like nearness. The road is open, the access is free: God meets us, and invites us to meet him. He waits to speak with us, as a man speaks with his friend.*

CHARLES SPURGEON, "OUR LORD'S ENTRANCE WITHIN THE VEIL"[12]

## WELCOME [READ ON YOUR OWN]

Not all artists use a hammer, chisel, paintbrush, or palette to create their works. Some instead rely on a small sliver of pointed steel—a needle. These craftspeople deal not in wood, stone, or canvas but in wool, cotton, silk, and other materials turned into fabrics. With this material in hand, these designers create all kinds of garments for all kinds of purposes and for all shapes and sizes of people. They even create fashion trends with their works.

Fabrics made in the first century were a much simpler affair. Most were created from hand-spun wool or linen through a process that involved spinning, weaving, and sewing. Making clothes was generally a domestic activity, often undertaken by women, with each garment custom-made for the wearer. The standard attire worn by men in Israel included a tunic-like undergarment, a longer tunic over it (often held in place with a belt), and possibly a robe or cloak over it. Jesus himself would have worn this simple attire.

Yet there was something unique about the inner tunic that Jesus wore. It was "seamless, woven in one piece from top to bottom" (John 19:23), which made it valuable enough for the Roman soldiers to cast lots for it.

This description of Jesus' tunic is reminiscent of the seamless garment the high priest wore in Old Testament times (see Exodus 28:31–32). The Gospels also mention another unique fabric related to Israel's priesthood: the veil that hung in the temple. When Jesus died, this curtain "was torn in two from top to bottom" (Matthew 27:51). He would now be our high priest, and there would no longer be a barrier between God and his people.

## CONNECT [15 MINUTES]

Get the session started by discussing one or both of the following questions as a group:

- Briefly share your experience of the Lenten practice you did last week. The focus of this practice was confession. What was it like to reflect on your life, to practice confession, and to receive God's forgiveness?

— or —

- What was the most helpful watchword you identified in your daily Scripture reading? How did God use it to challenge, encourage, or comfort you?

# WATCH [20 MINUTES]

Now watch the video for this session. Below is an outline of the key points covered during the teaching. Record any key concepts that stand out to you.

## OUTLINE

**I. What are you wearing?**

   **A.** Morally, how we "dress" ourselves—the ethics and convictions we embrace—shapes our attitude, choices, and behavior. It indicates to others who we really are . . . on the inside.

   **B.** Seats aren't available at God's table for the sloppy. But who among us is anything but? Yes, the standard for sitting at God's table is high. But the love of God for his children is higher.

   **C.** As we prepare to enter the "stage" of life and live out the part that God wants us to play, it might be a good idea to look in the mirror and ask the question, "What clothes am I wearing?"

   **D.** Jesus not only offered us his own robe but also invited us into his Father's presence.

**II. Between us and God**

   **A.** Jesus hasn't left us with an unapproachable God. Yes, God is holy. Yes, we are sinful. But Jesus is our mediator. He was the curtain between us and God, and his flesh was torn for you and me.

   **B.** There is a "curtain" in our hearts. Our guilty conscience becomes a curtain that separates us from God. As a result, we hide from our Master. Jesus came to remove that curtain.

**III. Clothed in righteousness**

   **A.** Jesus took off his robe of seamless perfection and assumed the wardrobe of indignity, nakedness, and failure. Worst of all, he wore the indignity of sin.

   **B.** Somewhere, sometime, somehow, we got tangled up in garbage and we've been avoiding God. We've allowed a veil of guilt to come between us and our heavenly Father.

   **C.** We came to the cross dressed in sin, but we leave dressed in the "coat of his strong love" (Isaiah 59:17 NCV), girded with a belt of "goodness and fairness" (Isaiah 11:5 NCV), and clothed in "garments of salvation" (Isaiah 61:10). Indeed, we leave dressed in Christ himself!

D. God has spotted us, heard us, and invited us. What once separated us from his presence has been removed. Nothing remains between us and God but an open door.

E. How could this be? In a word, because someone opened the curtain. Someone tore down the veil. Something happened in the death of Christ that opened the door for you and me.

## NOTES

## DISCUSS [35 MINUTES]

Discuss what you just watched by answering the following questions.

1. For the Jews of Jesus' day, God's presence resided solely in the temple—specifically, in the innermost room of the temple called the holy of holies or the Most Holy Place. Because God was holy and his people were not, thick curtains provided a barrier of separation between them.[13] It would thus have been unthinkable for the Jews of that time to believe that God's presence could reside *outside* the temple. In what ways do you recognize remnants of this mindset among people today? What form does it take?

2. How does the parallel between the temple curtain and Jesus' body help you understand what Christ's death on the cross really accomplished? What might have been less clear or harder to understand if the temple curtain had not been torn?

3. What comes to mind when you imagine yourself stepping into the Most Holy Place in the temple? In what ways does imagining yourself there physically shift your perspective on what it means to access God's presence in your everyday life?

4. Author and pastor Eugene Peterson elaborates on what direct access to God's presence really means for us:

> The shock is nothing less than seismic to be told that the first thing that happened when Jesus died on the cross was that "the curtain of the temple was torn in two, from top to bottom." . . . What happened? The Holy Place is now Every Place. The Holy One of God is contemporary With Us. His time is our time. There is no more separation between there and here, then and now, sacred and secular. . . . The death of Jesus on the cross open[s] up "a new and

living way" by which we can live an integrated life.[14]

We can live an *integrated* life. The challenge is that we sometimes instead default to a *dis-integrated*, or compartmentalized, life with God. How would you describe the purpose of the "curtain" or separation barrier this compartmentalization represents in your life? What integration might you be shielding yourself from?

5. Guilt is a curtain of the heart we sometimes use to shield ourselves from God's presence. How would you describe God's invitation to you when you use guilt as a shield? At those times, what might choosing an integrated life—dropping the curtain—require of you?

## RESPOND [10 MINUTES]

Reflect on what you've learned and experienced together in this study so far.

- How has learning about the gifts of the crown of thorns, the nails, and the robe impacted you and your relationship with God?

- Since the first session, what shifts have you noticed in yourself in terms of how you relate to the group? For example, do you feel more or less guarded, understood, challenged, encouraged, connected?

## PRAY [10 MINUTES]

Take a moment to give thanks for the gift of the robe. Ask God to remove any distractions that take your gaze away from Jesus' sacrifice. Record any prayer requests or praises so you and your group members can pray about them in the week ahead.

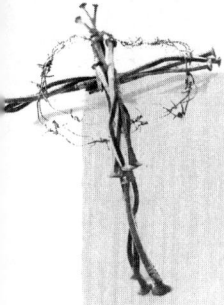

# LENTEN PRACTICE

*By faith in Christ you are in direct relationship with God.*
*Your baptism in Christ was not just washing you up for a fresh*
*start. It also involved dressing you in an adult faith wardrobe—*
*Christ's life, the fulfillment of God's original promise.*

GALATIANS 3:26–27 MSG

In the group time, you saw how Jesus not only offered you his own robe of perfection but also invited you into God's presence. Jesus wore your sin so you could wear his righteousness, and you leave the cross dressed in the "coat of his strong love" (Isaiah 59:17 NCV). Through his death, Christ destroyed the barrier that once separated you from God, and you now have direct access to God's presence. The challenge and opportunity you have each day is to live in conscious awareness of God's presence. Author and pastor A. W. Tozer writes:

> God wills that we should push on into his Presence and live our whole life there. This is to be known to us in conscious experience. It is more than a doctrine to be held, it is a life to be enjoyed every moment of every day. . . . The Presence of God is the central fact of Christianity. At the heart of the Christian message is God himself waiting for his redeemed children to push in to conscious awareness of his Presence.[15]

This week, you will use your daily routine of getting dressed as a prompt to "put on the Lord Jesus Christ" (Romans 13:14 NASB) and increase your awareness of God's presence with you. As you get ready for the day, allow each piece of clothing to serve as a reminder that you are dressed in the "coat of his strong love" and have access to God's presence. If you find it helpful, write the following prayer from A. W. Tozer on a card or Post-it note and place it on a mirror or in a closet or dresser drawer: *"Lord, increase my curiosity and help me to know You so intimately that I am especially, specifically, consciously aware of Your Presence throughout the day."*[16]

Here is a general overview of what each day will look like:

- As you get ready, allow each piece of clothing you put on to serve as a reminder that you are dressed in the "coat of his strong love" and have access to God's presence. Then, in God's presence, reflect on these questions:

  - *In the last twenty-four hours, when was I aware of God's presence?*
  - *When do I wish I had been consciously aware of God's presence?*

- Next, ask the Lord to speak to you through what you are about to read. Go over the Scripture passages for the morning slowly and prayerfully, paying attention to anything that sparks a connection between the text and your life. These are your **watchwords** for the day. They might be a promise, a word of wisdom, an admonition, a comfort, or an encouragement.

- Read your morning watchwords again, receiving what you read as God's words especially for you. Then reflect on the following questions:

  - *What do I sense God is saying to me?*
  - *If I took these words seriously, how would I respond?*

- Sometime later in the day, read the evening psalm slowly and prayerfully, again paying attention to any words, phrases, or verses that stand out to you. Write down your evening **watchwords** for this psalm.

- Read these watchwords again, and then reflect on the following questions:

  - *What do I sense God is saying to me?*
  - *If I took these words seriously, how would I respond?*

- Close by asking God to help you to "put on Christ" each day this week (and every day that follows) and to be consciously aware of his presence with you. Invite him to use your watchwords to continue speaking to you throughout the rest of the day. Write down any other observations about your experience of reading God's Word and listening for his voice.

- At the end of the week, review your daily reflections and observations. What stands out most to you about what God is saying to you? Write your observations in the space provided or in your journal.

Bring your notes to the next group gathering if you are doing the study with others, as you will have a chance to talk about your observations at the beginning of the session.

# DAY 15

## PREPARATION

As you get ready for the day, allow each piece of clothing you put on to serve as a reminder that you are dressed in the "coat of his strong love" and have access to God's presence.

## REFLECTION

*Lord, in the last twenty-four hours, when was I consciously aware of your presence? When do I wish that I had been consciously aware of your presence?*

## MORNING READING

Remember each day to ask the Lord to speak to you through what you are about to read. Pay attention to any words, phrases, or verses that stand out to you.

- **Psalm:** Psalms 93; 95
- **Epistle:** Romans 8:1–10
- **Old Testament:** Genesis 44:1–17
- **Gospel:** John 5:25–29

**Watchwords** (anything that sparks a connection between the text and your life):

*What do I sense God is saying to me? If I took these words seriously, how would I respond?*

## EVENING READING

Once again, ask the Lord to speak to you through what you are about to read.

> **Psalm:** Psalms 34; 96

**Watchwords:**

*What do I sense God is saying to me? If I took these words seriously, how would I respond?*

## CLOSE

Close each day by asking God to help you to "put on Christ" every day this week (and every day that follows) and to be consciously aware of his presence with you. Journal any other observations about your experience of reading God's Word and listening for his voice.

# DAY 16

## REFLECTION

*Lord, in the last twenty-four hours, when was I consciously aware of your presence? When do I wish that I had been consciously aware of your presence?*

## MORNING READING

- **Psalm:** Psalm 80
- **Epistle:** 1 Corinthians 7:25–31
- **Old Testament:** Genesis 44:18–34
- **Gospel:** Mark 7:1–37

**Watchwords:**

*What do I sense God is saying to me? If I took these words seriously, how would I respond?*

## EVENING READING

- **Psalm:** Psalm 79

**Watchwords:**

*What do I sense God is saying to me? If I took these words seriously, how would I respond?*

# DAY 17

## REFLECTION

*Lord, in the last twenty-four hours, when was I consciously aware of your presence? When do I wish that I had been consciously aware of your presence?*

## MORNING READING

- **Psalm:** Psalm 78:1–39
- **Epistle:** 1 Corinthians 7:32–40
- **Old Testament:** Genesis 45:1–15
- **Gospel:** Mark 8:1–21

**Watchwords:**

*What do I sense God is saying to me? If I took these words seriously, how would I respond?*

## EVENING READING

- **Psalm:** Psalm 78:40–72

**Watchwords:**

*What do I sense God is saying to me? If I took these words seriously, how would I respond?*

# Day 18

## REFLECTION

*Lord, in the last twenty-four hours, when was I consciously aware of your presence? When do I wish that I had been consciously aware of your presence?*

## MORNING READING

- **Psalm:** Psalm 119:97–120
- **Epistle:** 1 Corinthians 8:1–13
- **Old Testament:** Genesis 45:16–28
- **Gospel:** Mark 8:22–33

**Watchwords:**

*What do I sense God is saying to me? If I took these words seriously, how would I respond?*

## EVENING READING

- **Psalm:** Psalms 81; 82

**Watchwords:**

*What do I sense God is saying to me? If I took these words seriously, how would I respond?*

# DAY 19

## REFLECTION

*Lord, in the last twenty-four hours, when was I consciously aware of your presence? When do I wish that I had been consciously aware of your presence?*

## MORNING READING

- **Psalm:** Psalm 42
- **Epistle:** 1 Corinthians 9:1–15
- **Old Testament:** Genesis 46:1–7, 28–34
- **Gospel:** Mark 8:34–9:13

**Watchwords:**

*What do I sense God is saying to me? If I took these words seriously, how would I respond?*

## EVENING READING

- **Psalm:** Psalms 85; 86

**Watchwords:**

*What do I sense God is saying to me? If I took these words seriously, how would I respond?*

# DAY 20

## REFLECTION

*Lord, in the last twenty-four hours, when was I consciously aware of your presence? When do I wish that I had been consciously aware of your presence?*

## MORNING READING

- **Psalm:** Psalm 88
- **Epistle:** 1 Corinthians 9:16–27
- **Old Testament:** Genesis 47:1–26
- **Gospel:** Mark 9:14–29

Watchwords:

*What do I sense God is saying to me? If I took these words seriously, how would I respond?*

## EVENING READING

- **Psalm:** Psalm 91

Watchwords:

*What do I sense God is saying to me? If I took these words seriously, how would I respond?*

# DAY 21

## REFLECTION

*Lord, in the last twenty-four hours, when was I consciously aware of your presence? When do I wish that I had been consciously aware of your presence?*

## MORNING READING

- **Psalm:** Psalms 87; 90
- **Epistle:** 1 Corinthians 10:1–13
- **Old Testament:** Genesis 47:27–48:7
- **Gospel:** Mark 9:30–50

**Watchwords:**

*What do I sense God is saying to me? If I took these words seriously, how would I respond?*

## EVENING READING

- **Psalm:** Psalm 136

**Watchwords:**

*What do I sense God is saying to me? If I took these words seriously, how would I respond?*

# Week in Review

Review the daily reflections and observations that you recorded during the course of this week. *What stands out most to you about what God is saying to you?*

Read chapters 11–13 in *He Chose the Nails* before the next group gathering. Use the space below to make note of anything that stands out to you or encourages you.

| | |
|---|---|
| **BEFORE GROUP MEETING** | Read chapters 11–13 in *He Chose the Nails* <br> Read the Welcome section (page 66) |
| **GROUP MEETING** | Discuss the Connect questions <br> Watch the video teaching for session 4 <br> Discuss the questions that follow as a group <br> Do the closing exercise and pray (pages 66–70) |
| **LENTEN PRACTICES:** <br> DAYS 22 TO 28 | Complete the daily Lenten practices (pages 71–82) |
| **CATCH UP AND READ AHEAD** <br> (BEFORE WEEK 5 GROUP MEETING) | Complete the Week in Review (page 83) <br> Read chapters 14–15 in *He Chose the Nails* |

# He Chose to Love Us Forever

*This is how we know what love is:*
*Jesus Christ laid down his life for us.*

1 JOHN 3:16

*To follow Jesus implies that we enter into a*
*way of life that is given character and shape*
*and direction by the one who calls us.*

EUGENE H. PETERSON,
*THE JESUS WAY*[17]

## WELCOME [READ ON YOUR OWN]

There is one gift of Easter that is especially well-known to Christians today. It is the symbol of Easter itself: the *cross*. In truth, there is perhaps no more famous construction made of wood in the history of humankind. Yet it is also one that took no great carpentry skill nor mastery to create. In fact, many scholars actually believe it was just a simple rough-hewn wooden construction that was quickly put together by the Roman soldiers themselves.

The Gospels do not state what type of wood was used for Jesus' cross. However, common choices would have included olive, oak, and pine, as these were fairly abundant in the region and known for their durability and strength. It is believed that in situations where the place of execution was established, the vertical portion of the cross was permanently fixed into the ground. The condemned, meanwhile, was forced to carry the horizontal crossbar to the execution site. Upon arrival, the soldiers would nail the person's wrists to the crossbar, hoist it up, attach it to the fixed vertical beam, and then nail the person's feet to that beam.[18]

The cross afforded the Romans an effective, efficient, public, humiliating, and incredibly brutal means of execution. The design couldn't be simpler. One beam horizontal; the other vertical. One reaches out, like God's love. The other reaches up, as does God's holiness. The cross is the intersection. It is where God forgave humanity of their sin without lowering his standards. Seen in this light, the cross of Jesus is nothing less than the work of a master carpenter. It is a gift that is given to all who put their faith in the sacrifice that he made.

## CONNECT [15 MINUTES]

Get the session started by discussing one or both of the following questions as a group:

- Briefly share your experience of the Lenten practice you did last week. The focus of this practice was to use your daily routine of getting dressed as a prompt to be aware of God's presence. To what degree did the practice help to increase your awareness of God's presence throughout the day?

— or —

- What was the most helpful watchword you identified in your daily Scripture reading? How did God use it to challenge, encourage, or comfort you?

## WATCH [20 MINUTES]

Now watch the video for this session. Below is an outline of key points covered during the teaching. Record any key concepts that stand out to you.

### OUTLINE

I.  **Sanctification: the act of making or declaring something holy**
   A.  **Positional sanctification:** Christ's work for us. We are given a prize not because of what we do but because of who we know.
   B.  **Progressive sanctification:** Christ's work in us. We are continuously transformed by God.
   C.  Neglect the first and you grow fearful. Neglect the second and you grow lazy. Both are essential gifts from God. Both are seen in the moistened dirt at the base of the cross of Christ.

II. **The cross: the symbol of our faith**
   A.  The cross is the universal symbol of Christianity. The design couldn't be simpler: one beam represents the width of God's love and the other reflects the height of his holiness.
   B.  The cross is the intersection. It is where God forgave his children without lowering his standards. It is where God put our sin on his Son and punished it there. As boldly as the center beam proclaims God's holiness, the crossbeam declares his love.
   C.  The sin is punished, but we are safe in the shadow of the cross. We were "made holy through the sacrifice Christ made in his body once and for all time" (Hebrews 10:10 NCV).

III. **An elementary question: the work is complete**
   A.  We are positionally sanctified—the achievement of Jesus' blood is credited to us. We are also progressively sanctified—his work in us is ongoing.
   B.  We can't be more saved than we were the day we accepted Christ's sacrifice on the cross and received salvation. But we can grow in that salvation.
   C.  Because of God's love for us, we can engrave in our hearts the truth that Jesus is "the Lamb of God, who takes away the sin of the world" (John 1:29).
   D.  Because of God's love, the blood of Christ does not just cover, conceal, postpone, or diminish our sins but *takes away* our sins once and for all time. Jesus allows our mistakes to be lost in his perfection.

## NOTES

## DISCUSS [35 MINUTES]

Discuss what you just watched by answering the following questions.

1. The apostle Paul provides a beautiful description of God's work on the cross when he writes, "You were washed, you were sanctified, you were justified in the name of the Lord Jesus Christ and by the Spirit of our God" (1 Corinthians 6:11). Paul stresses the miracle of what God did for us on the cross with three distinct Greek words:

   *apolousasthe* (washed): to be washed entirely (not just a part), especially the removal of dirt; spiritually cleansed and purified by God.

   *hēgiasthēte* (sanctified): made holy, consecrated, set apart for a purpose.

   *edikaiōthēte* (justified): declared righteous, not guilty (in a legal sense); approved by God and conforming to God's standard.[19]

   How would you describe the journey that brought you to the cross?

2. As you reflect on your experience of surrendering your life to Christ, which of Paul's three words in 1 Corinthians 6:11 do you relate to the most? Why that word?

3. Paul beautifully acknowledged the reality of progressive sanctification—the expectation that we are continuously transformed by Christ—when he wrote, "The Lord—who is the Spirit—makes us more and more like him as we are changed into his glorious image" (2 Corinthians 3:18 NLT). The root of the Greek word Paul uses for *changed* is *metamorphoō*, which is the source of the English word *metamorphosis*, meaning a profound change that happens through growth. The kind of life-change metamorphosis implies is radical—from one form into another—but it is also gradual. What makes this kind of radical-gradual spiritual growth so uniquely challenging for you?

4. What desires or hopes does the promise of metamorphosis stir in you? For example, in what ways do you long for your life to be brighter, more beautiful?

5. Progressive sanctification includes the expectation not only of growth but also of an increasing aversion to and freedom from sin. Paul uses the image of light to help us understand what living out our salvation in this way requires: "Live as children of light—for the fruit of the light is found in all that is good and right and true" (Ephesians 5:8–9 NRSV). Paul could have used the phrase "people of light" instead of "children of light." What nuances might his use of *children* suggest about what living in light requires of us?

## RESPOND [10 MINUTES]

Take a moment to reflect on what you've learned and experienced together in this study so far.

- Jesus demonstrated his love for us on the cross, but his love didn't stop there. Every day, he invites us to receive his love anew and to be changed by it. As you continue to journey through Lent to Easter, in what ways or in what areas of life are you most aware of your need to receive God's love?

- How do you hope (or fear) you might be changed by that love? Why do you have these specific hopes (or fears)?

## PRAY [10 MINUTES]

Take a moment to give thanks for the gift of the cross. Ask God to remove any distractions that take your gaze away from Jesus' sacrifice. Record any prayer requests or praises so you and your group members can pray about them in the week ahead.

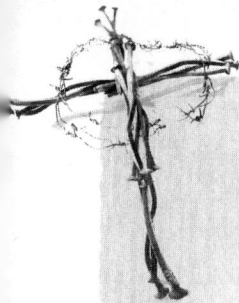

# LENTEN PRACTICE

*And so we are transfigured much like the Messiah, our
lives gradually becoming brighter and more beautiful as
God enters our lives and we become like him.*

2 CORINTHIANS 3:18 MSG

In the group time, you learned about two kinds of sanctification: positional sanctification (God's work for us) and progressive sanctification (God's work in us). Progressive sanctification includes all the ways we grow to become more like Christ. It also includes the expectation of an increasing aversion to sin. The challenge is that in our efforts to avoid sin, it's possible to give sin more space in our lives rather than less. Author and pastor John Ortberg writes:

> Many Christians expend so much energy and worry trying not to sin. The goal is not to try to sin less. In all your efforts to keep from sinning, what are you focusing on? Sin. God wants you to focus on him.[20]

The alternative to expending too much energy on trying not to sin is to switch our focus from sin to God, and to the good, which is how Dallas Willard describes one of the key characteristics of children of light: "[They are] mainly governed by the pull of the good. Their energy is not invested in not doing what is wrong, but in doing what is good."[21]

This week, you will continue to prepare your heart for Easter by shifting your focus from trying not to sin to being "governed by the pull of the good." You will begin by identifying an area in which you feel vulnerable to doing what is wrong or behaving in a regrettable way. The context might be a personal struggle, a difficult relationship, or a challenging circumstance. This situation will be your focus for seeking to be governed by the good this week. If you find it helpful, write a reminder on a Post-it note. For example, "Live as a child of light," "Focus on the pull of the good," or "Lord, give me the desire and the power to do what pleases you."

Here is a general overview of what each day will look like:

- Begin in the morning with a brief time of silence (one to two minutes). For the first half of the week, you will then reflect on these questions:

  - *How was I governed by the pull of the good yesterday?*
  - *How did I fail to be governed by the pull of the good yesterday?*

- For the second half of the week, you will reflect on these questions:

  - *Where am I vulnerable to doing what is wrong or regrettable today?*
  - *How might I invest my energy in doing what is good instead?*

- Next, ask the Lord to speak to you through what you are about to read. Go over the Scripture passages for the morning slowly and prayerfully, paying attention to anything that sparks a connection between the text and your life These are your **watchwords** for the day. They might be a promise, a word of wisdom, an admonition, a comfort, or an encouragement.

- Read your morning watchwords again, receiving what you read as God's words especially for you. Then reflect on the following questions:

  - *What do I sense God is saying to me?*
  - *If I took these words seriously, how would I respond?*

- Sometime later in the day, read the evening psalm slowly and prayerfully, again paying attention to any words, phrases, or verses that stand out to you. Write down your evening **watchwords** for this psalm.

- Read these watchwords again, and then reflect on the following questions:

  - *What do I sense God is saying to me?*
  - *If I took these words seriously, how would I respond?*

- Close by asking God to give you "the desire and the power to do what pleases him" (Philippians 2:13 NLT). Invite him to use your watchwords to continue speaking to you throughout the rest of the day. Write down any other observations or reflections regarding your experience.

- At the end of the week, review your daily reflections and observations. What stands out most to you about what God is saying to you? Write your observations in the space provided or in your journal.

Bring your notes to the next group gathering if you are doing the study with others, as you will have a chance to talk about your observations at the beginning of the session.

# DAY 22

## PREPARATION

Begin each day with a time of silence (one to two minutes). Be still for just a few moments to free your mind from distractions and worries so you can focus on your time with the Lord.

## REFLECTION

*Lord, how was I governed by the pull of the good yesterday? How did I fail to be governed by the pull of the good yesterday?*

## MORNING READING

Remember each day to ask the Lord to speak to you through what you are about to read. Pay attention to any words, phrases, or verses that stand out to you.

| | |
|---|---|
| • **Psalm:** Psalms 66; 95 | • **Old Testament:** Genesis 48:8–22 |
| • **Epistle:** Romans 8:11–25 | • **Gospel:** John 6:27–40 |

**Watchwords** (anything that sparks a connection between the text and your life):

*What do I sense God is saying to me? If I took these words seriously, how would I respond?*

## EVENING READING

Once again, ask the Lord to speak to you through what you are about to read.

> • **Psalm:** Psalms 19; 46

**Watchwords:**

*What do I sense God is saying to me? If I took these words seriously, how would I respond?*

## CLOSE

Close each day by asking God to give you "the desire and the power to do what pleases him" (Philippians 2:13 NLT). Journal any other observations about your experience of reading God's Word and listening for his voice.

# DAY 23

## REFLECTION

*Lord, how was I governed by the pull of the good yesterday? How did I fail to be governed by the pull of the good yesterday?*

## MORNING READING

- **Psalm:** Psalm 89:1–18
- **Epistle:** 1 Corinthians 10:14–11:1
- **Old Testament:** Genesis 49:1–28
- **Gospel:** Mark 10:1–16

**Watchwords:**

*What do I sense God is saying to me? If I took these words seriously, how would I respond?*

## EVENING READING

- **Psalm:** Psalm 89:19–52

**Watchwords:**

*What do I sense God is saying to me? If I took these words seriously, how would I respond?*

# DAY 24

## REFLECTION

*Lord, how was I governed by the pull of the good yesterday? How did I fail to be governed by the pull of the good yesterday?*

## MORNING READING

- **Psalm:** Psalms 97; 99
- **Epistle:** 1 Corinthians 11:17–34
- **Old Testament:** Genesis 49:29–50:14
- **Gospel:** Mark 10:17–31

Watchwords:

*What do I sense God is saying to me? If I took these words seriously, how would I respond?*

## EVENING READING

- **Psalm:** Psalm 94

Watchwords:

*What do I sense God is saying to me? If I took these words seriously, how would I respond?*

# DAY 25

## REFLECTION

*Lord, how was I governed by the pull of the good yesterday? How did I fail to be governed by the pull of the good yesterday?*

## MORNING READING

- **Psalm:** Psalms 101; 109
- **Epistle:** 1 Corinthians 12:1–11
- **Old Testament:** Genesis 50:15–26
- **Gospel:** Mark 10:32–46

**Watchwords:**

*What do I sense God is saying to me? If I took these words seriously, how would I respond?*

## EVENING READING

- **Psalm:** Psalm 119:121–144

**Watchwords:**

*What do I sense God is saying to me? If I took these words seriously, how would I respond?*

# DAY 26

## REFLECTION

*Where am I vulnerable to doing what is wrong or regrettable today? How might I invest my energy in doing what is good instead?*

## MORNING READING

- **Psalm:** Psalms 5; 10
- **Epistle:** 1 Corinthians 12:12–26
- **Old Testament:** Exodus 1:6–22
- **Gospel:** Mark 11:1–25

**Watchwords:**

*What do I sense God is saying to me? If I took these words seriously, how would I respond?*

## EVENING READING

- **Psalm:** Psalm 37

**Watchwords:**

*What do I sense God is saying to me? If I took these words seriously, how would I respond?*

# DAY 27

## REFLECTION

*Where am I vulnerable to doing what is wrong or regrettable today? How might I invest my energy in doing what is good instead?*

## MORNING READING

- **Psalm:** Psalm 102
- **Epistle:** 1 Corinthians 12:27–31
- **Old Testament:** Exodus 2:1–22
- **Gospel:** Mark 11:27–12:12

**Watchwords:**

*What do I sense God is saying to me? If I took these words seriously, how would I respond?*

## EVENING READING

- **Psalm:** Psalm 92

**Watchwords:**

*What do I sense God is saying to me? If I took these words seriously, how would I respond?*

# DAY 28

## REFLECTION

*Where am I vulnerable to doing what is wrong or regrettable today? How might I invest my energy in doing what is good instead?*

## MORNING READING

- **Psalm:** Psalm 107:33–43
- **Epistle:** 1 Corinthians 13:1–13
- **Old Testament:** Exodus 2:23–3:15
- **Gospel:** Mark 12:13–44

Watchwords:

*What do I sense God is saying to me? If I took these words seriously, how would I respond?*

## EVENING READING

- **Psalm:** Psalm 33

Watchwords:

*What do I sense God is saying to me? If I took these words seriously, how would I respond?*

# WEEK IN REVIEW

Review the daily reflections and observations that you recorded during the course of this week. *What stands out most to you about what God is saying to you?*

Read chapters 14–15 in *He Chose the Nails* before the next group gathering. Use the space below to make note of anything that stands out to you or encourages you.

| | |
|---|---|
| **BEFORE GROUP MEETING** | Read chapters 14–15 in *He Chose the Nails* <br> Read the Welcome section (page 86) |
| **GROUP MEETING** | Discuss the Connect questions <br> Watch the video teaching for session 5 <br> Discuss the questions that follow as a group <br> Do the closing exercise and pray (pages 86–90) |
| **LENTEN PRACTICES:** <br> DAYS 29 TO 35 | Complete the daily Lenten practices (pages 91–102) |
| **CATCH UP AND READ AHEAD** <br> (IF MEETING NEXT WEEK) | Read the Final Words in *He Chose the Nails* <br> Complete the Week in Review (page 103) |

# HE CHOSE TO GIVE US VICTORY

*Overwhelming victory is ours through Christ, who loved us.*

ROMANS 8:37 NLT

*[Jesus] came in the flesh and he suffered all of the things that people suffer in the flesh. He does this so that we can go with him to the cross, and we can participate in the brokenness of this life so that we can see and enter into the resurrection of Jesus and be a part of that. . . . It's through death that we enter into the victory that is beyond death.*

DALLAS WILLARD, "A CONVERSATION ON PAIN AND SUFFERING"[22]

## WELCOME [READ ON YOUR OWN]

Most of us don't like to think about our funeral, much less discuss it. Death signals the end of our time on earth. It's a time of sadness for those we leave behind. This was certainly the case, at first, for the disciples of Jesus. When he was crucified by the Roman soldiers, and his body taken down from the cross and laid in the tomb of Joseph of Arimathea, it must have seemed as if everything they had hoped for in their promised Messiah had come to an end.

This tomb, in keeping with Jewish burial practices of the time, was carved out of rock. It was a "new tomb"—meaning no one had been buried in it before—and had "a big stone" that was rolled "in front of the entrance" (Matthew 27:60). The doorway was low, given that Peter and Mary Magdalene had to bend over to look inside (see John 20:5, 11). The fact that Mary saw two angels in white "seated where Jesus' body had been" (verse 12) indicates the interior was likely a single chamber with a bench or shelf where Jesus' body was laid.

In other words . . . the tomb itself was not all that extraordinary. Many Jewish families owned tombs like it to bury their deceased. What *was* extraordinary is that this tomb did not remain occupied. Three days after Jesus' death, it was discovered empty by Mary Magdalene and other women who went to anoint Christ's body—and by the disciples Peter and John. The tomb, at first, appeared to them to be a sign of hopelessness and defeat. But what it became—for both them and us today—is a sign of Jesus' greatest victory over sin and death.

## CONNECT [15 MINUTES]

Get the session started by discussing one or both of the following questions as a group:

- Briefly share your experience of the Lenten practice you did last week. The focus of this practice was to shift your concentration from trying hard *not* to sin to being "governed by the pull of the good" instead. What did you find most challenging about shifting your focus in this way?

— or —

- What was the most helpful watchword you identified in your daily Scripture reading? How did God use it to challenge, encourage, or comfort you?

# WATCH [20 MINUTES]

Now watch the video for this session. Below is an outline of the key points covered during the teaching. Record any key concepts that stand out to you.

## OUTLINE

I. **The Suffering Servant**

   A. The trio of dying men groaned as they hung on the crosses. But as the minutes became hours, the groans diminished. And then, just before Jesus died, he asked for something to drink.

   B. Jesus didn't have to suffer thirst to the level he did. Six hours earlier, he had been offered drink. But he refused myrrh and gall. He refused to be stupefied by the drugs. Why?

   C. Jesus knew we'd face thirst. If not a thirst for water, a thirst for truth. The truth we glean from this is that Jesus understands. And because he understands, we can come to him.

II. **Linger at the cross**

   A. John tells us that after the drink was offered, and the afternoon dawn broke, Jesus spoke a final time. "It is finished," he said (John 19:30). With his head bowed, he gave his final breath.

   B. John had no way of knowing on that Friday what you and I now know. He didn't know Friday's tragedy would be Sunday's triumph.

   C. God had taken the wrappings of death and had made them the picture of life. Could he do something similar in our lives? Could he take what today is a token of tragedy—like a beat-up old trumpet—and turn it into a symbol of triumph?

III. **Go first to God**

   A. We all face tragedy. But could God use those tragedies for something good? How far can we go with verses like Romans 8:28: "In everything God works for the good of those who love him" (NCV)? John would tell you God can turn any tragedy into a triumph, if only you wait and watch.

   B. For the cross of Christ to be the cross of our lives, we need to bring something to the hill. We can bring our bad moments and mad moments: bad habits, selfish moods, white lies, binges, and bigotries.

**C.** The first step after a stumble must be in the direction of the cross. "If we confess our sins to God, he can always be trusted to forgive us and take our sins away" (1 John 1:9 CEV).

**D.** If God can change the disciples' lives through a tragedy such as the cross and the tomb, could it be he will use a tragedy to change yours? As hard as it may be to believe, you could be only a Saturday away from a resurrection.

## NOTES

## DISCUSS [35 MINUTES]

Discuss what you just watched by answering the following questions.

1. The victory accomplished through Christ's death and resurrection is sometimes referred to as the "paschal mystery." The word *paschal* comes from the Greek word for *Passover*, the Jewish remembrance of when the angel of death "passed over" the Hebrew families prior to their exodus from Egypt (see Exodus 12:13, 23). Eugene Peterson comments on God's paschal work in our lives when he writes, "All suffering, all pain, all emptiness, all disappointment is seed: sow it in God and he will, finally, bring a crop of joy from it."[23] What three words or phrases would you use to describe the life of the seed before death? What three words or phrases would you use to describe the life that follows death?

2. If we think of the hardships and losses of this life as seeds, we have at least three options for what we can do with them: (1) cling to our seeds and refuse to sow them; (2) sow our seeds in God; or (3) sow our seeds in something other than God. In practical terms, how would you describe what it means to follow through on each option? Which comes closest to describing your tendency when you are in a season of hardship?

3. We all face tragedy and hardships, but the promise of Scripture is that God is at work to bring victory and new life. Paul writes, "We know that God causes everything to work together for the good of those who love God and are called according to his purpose. . . . Can anything ever separate us from Christ's love? . . . No, despite all these things, overwhelming victory is ours through Christ, who loved us" (Romans 8:28, 35, 37 NLT). Based on how Paul describes victory, how would you describe its opposite, defeat? In other words, how might we refuse or thwart our victory, perhaps when we are suffering?

4. Jesus said, "Here on earth you will have many trials and sorrows. But take heart, because I have overcome the world" (John 16:33 NLT). If living in victory is possible even in the midst of our "many trials and sorrows," how would you describe what that victory is?

5. Think about Paul's words: "In everything God works for the good of those who love him" (Romans 8:28 NCV). Remove the word *everything* and replace it with whatever symbolizes a tragedy or hardship in your life. For example, "In hospital stays God works for the good." How would you complete the sentence? "In _____ God works for the good"?

## RESPOND [10 MINUTES]

Take a moment to reflect on what you've learned and experienced throughout this study.

- In the first session, you considered how Lent is a season that prepares us to return to God with all our heart. In what ways, if any, did this perspective change how you thought about or experienced Lent this year?

- Overall, how would you describe your experience of the Lenten practices? To what degree did they help you to prepare spiritually for Easter? How have you recognized God's work among you as a group throughout the study?

## PRAY [10 MINUTES]

Take a moment to give thanks for the gift of salvation. Ask God to remove any distractions that take your gaze away from Jesus' sacrifice. Record any prayer requests or praises so you and your group members can continue to pray about them in the weeks ahead.

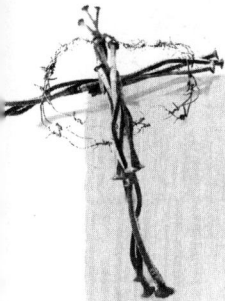

# LENTEN PRACTICE

*Listen carefully: Unless a grain of wheat is buried in the ground,*
*dead to the world, it is never any more than a grain of wheat.*
*But if it is buried, it sprouts and reproduces itself many times over.*
*In the same way, anyone who holds on to life just as*
*it is destroys that life. But if you let it go, reckless in your love,*
*you'll have it forever, real and eternal.*

JOHN 12:24–25 MSG

Just as Jesus died, was buried, and rose again to new life, so God's transforming work in our lives often follows a paschal pattern. You touched on this idea in the group session when you discussed how we all need to bring something to Calvary, the hill where Christ was crucified:

> In order for the cross of Christ to be the cross of your life, you and I need to bring something to the hill. We have seen what Jesus brought. . . . Now we ask, what will we bring? . . . You can observe the cross and analyze the cross. You can read about it, even pray to it. But until you leave something there, you haven't embraced the cross.[24]

We can start with our *bad* moments and *mad* moments: selfish moods, self-defeating habits (of thought, feeling, or behavior), white lies, misuse of time, angry outbursts, binges, people-pleasing, mistakes, substance abuse, bitterness, cheating, mismanaging money, regret, gossip, neglect, bigotries, bad attitudes, pride, or slander. We can also bring our *anxious* moments to the hill: worries, fears, anxieties, and emotional struggles:

> Take your anxieties to the cross—literally. Next time you're worried about your health or house or finances or flights, take a mental trip up the hill. . . . Knowing all he did for you there, don't you think he'll look out for you here?[25]

The invitation this week is to embrace the cross—to leave something on the hill each day that you know you need to "die to" in order to receive new life. Choose an area of concern. It might be a specific issue (such as the previous examples of bad, mad, and anxious moments) or a difficult relationship or circumstance. Whatever the issue or situation, ask yourself, *What does letting go—leaving this at the hill—require of me in this moment?* Take a time-out to think about it—and then do it. Allow leaving that issue at the hill to determine your demeanor, your body language, your words, your actions. If helpful, write a reminder on a Post-it note or create some note that says: "Leave it at the hill."

Here is an overview of what each day will look like:

- Begin in the morning with a brief time of silence (one to two minutes). Then, in God's loving presence, reflect on these questions:

  ▸ *What was I able to leave at the hill yesterday?*
  ▸ *What do I need to leave at the hill today?*

- Next, ask the Lord to speak to you through what you are about to read. Go over the Scripture passages for the morning slowly and prayerfully, paying attention to anything that sparks a connection between the text and your life. These are your **watchwords** for the day. They might be a promise, a word of wisdom, an admonition, a comfort, or an encouragement.

- Read your morning watchwords again, receiving what you read as God's words especially for you. Then reflect on the following questions:

  ▸ *What do I sense God is saying to me?*
  ▸ *If I took these words seriously, how would I respond?*

- Sometime later in the day, read the evening psalm slowly and prayerfully, again paying attention to any words, phrases, or verses that stand out to you. Write down your evening **watchwords** for this psalm.

- Read these watchwords again, and then reflect on the following questions:

> ▸ *What do I sense God is saying to me?*
> ▸ *If I took these words seriously, how would I respond?*

- Close by asking God to help you trust him with everything you leave at the hill. Invite him to use your watchwords to continue speaking to you throughout the rest of the day. Write down any other observations about your experience of reading God's Word and listening for his voice.

- At the end of the week, review your daily reflections and observations. What stands out most to you about what God is saying to you? Write your observations in the space provided or in your journal.

If you are in a group and it is meeting next week, bring your notes to the gathering. If your group has concluded, consider sharing your observations and experiences from this week's practice with a friend or another member of the group one-on-one in the coming days.

# DAY 29

## PREPARATION

Begin each day with a time of silence (one to two minutes). Be still for just a few moments to free your mind from distractions and worries so you can focus on your time with the Lord.

## REFLECTION

*Lord, what was I able to leave at the hill yesterday? What do I need to leave at the hill today?*

## MORNING READING

Remember each day to ask the Lord to speak to you through what you are about to read. Pay attention to any words, phrases, or verses that stand out to you.

- **Psalm:** Psalms 67; 95
- **Epistle:** Romans 12:1–21
- **Old Testament:** Exodus 3:16–4:12
- **Gospel:** John 8:46–59

**Watchwords** (anything that sparks a connection between the text and your life):

*What do I sense God is saying to me? If I took these words seriously, how would I respond?*

## EVENING READING

Once again, ask the Lord to speak to you through what you are about to read.

- **Psalm:** Psalm 145

**Watchwords:**

*What do I sense God is saying to me? If I took these words seriously, how would I respond?*

## CLOSE

Close by asking God to help you trust him with everything you leave at the hill. Journal any other observations about your experience of reading God's Word and listening for his voice.

# DAY 30

## REFLECTION

*Lord, what was I able to leave at the hill yesterday? What do I need to leave at the hill today?*

## MORNING READING

- **Psalm:** Psalm 31
- **Epistle:** 1 Corinthians 14:1–19
- **Old Testament:** Exodus 4:13–31
- **Gospel:** Mark 13:1–20

**Watchwords:**

*What do I sense God is saying to me? If I took these words seriously, how would I respond?*

## EVENING READING

- **Psalm:** Psalm 35

**Watchwords:**

*What do I sense God is saying to me? If I took these words seriously, how would I respond?*

# DAY 31

## REFLECTION

*Lord, what was I able to leave at the hill yesterday? What do I need to leave at the hill today?*

## MORNING READING

- **Psalm:** Psalms 121; 122
- **Epistle:** 1 Corinthians 14:20-40
- **Old Testament:** Exodus 5:1–6:1
- **Gospel:** Mark 13:21-37

**Watchwords:**

*What do I sense God is saying to me? If I took these words seriously, how would I respond?*

## EVENING READING

- **Psalm:** Psalms 123; 124

**Watchwords:**

*What do I sense God is saying to me? If I took these words seriously, how would I respond?*

# DAY 32

## REFLECTION

*Lord, what was I able to leave at the hill yesterday? What do I need to leave at the hill today?*

## MORNING READING

- **Psalm:** Psalm 119:145–176
- **Epistle:** 2 Corinthians 2:14–3:18
- **Old Testament:** Exodus 7:8–24
- **Gospel:** Mark 14:1–26

**Watchwords:**

*What do I sense God is saying to me? If I took these words seriously, how would I respond?*

## EVENING READING

- **Psalm:** Psalms 125; 126; 128

**Watchwords:**

*What do I sense God is saying to me? If I took these words seriously, how would I respond?*

# DAY 33

## REFLECTION

*Lord, what was I able to leave at the hill yesterday? What do I need to leave at the hill today?*

## MORNING READING

- **Psalm:** Psalms 131; 132
- **Epistle:** 2 Corinthians 4:1–12
- **Old Testament:** Exodus 7:25–8:19
- **Gospel:** Mark 14:27–42

**Watchwords:**

*What do I sense God is saying to me? If I took these words seriously, how would I respond?*

## EVENING READING

- **Psalm:** Psalms 140; 142

**Watchwords:**

*What do I sense God is saying to me? If I took these words seriously, how would I respond?*

# DAY 34

## REFLECTION

*Lord, what was I able to leave at the hill yesterday? What do I need to leave at the hill today?*

## MORNING READING

- **Psalm:** Psalm 22
- **Epistle:** 2 Corinthians 4:13–5:10
- **Old Testament:** Exodus 9:13–35
- **Gospel:** Mark 14:43–65

**Watchwords:**

*What do I sense God is saying to me? If I took these words seriously, how would I respond?*

## EVENING READING

- **Psalm:** Psalms 141; 143

**Watchwords:**

*What do I sense God is saying to me? If I took these words seriously, how would I respond?*

# DAY 35

## REFLECTION

*Lord, what was I able to leave at the hill yesterday? What do I need to leave at the hill today?*

## MORNING READING

- **Psalm:** Psalms 137; 144
- **Epistle:** 2 Corinthians 5:11–21
- **Old Testament:** Exodus 10:21–11:10
- **Gospel:** Mark 14:66–15:39

Watchwords:

*What do I sense God is saying to me? If I took these words seriously, how would I respond?*

## EVENING READING

- **Psalm:** Psalm 43

Watchwords:

*What do I sense God is saying to me? If I took these words seriously, how would I respond?*

# WEEK IN REVIEW

Review the daily reflections and observations that you recorded during the course of this week. *What stands out most to you about what God is saying to you?*

Read the Final Words in *He Chose the Nails* if you are meeting with your group next week. Use the space below to make note of anything that stands out to you or encourages you.

| | |
|---|---|
| **BEFORE GROUP MEETING** | Read the Final Words in *He Chose the Nails* <br> Read the Welcome section (page 106) |
| **GROUP MEETING** | Discuss the Connect questions <br> Discuss the questions as a group <br> Do the closing exercise and pray (pages 106–110) |
| **LENTEN PRACTICES:** DAYS 36 TO 40 | Complete the daily Lenten practices (pages 111–120) |
| **WRAP IT UP** | Complete the Week in Review (page 121) <br> Connect with your group members about the next study that you want to go through together |

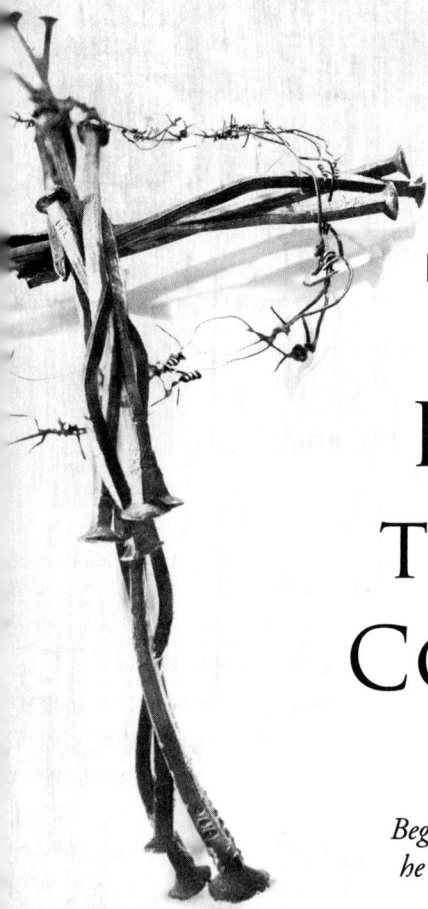

# HE CHOSE
# TO GIVE US
# CONFIDENCE

*Beginning with Moses and all the Prophets,*
*he explained to them what was said in all*
*the Scriptures concerning himself.*

LUKE 24:27

*Always, everywhere God is present, and always*
*he seeks to discover himself to each one.*

A. W. TOZER, *THE PURSUIT OF GOD*[26]

## WELCOME [READ ON YOUR OWN]

After Jesus' resurrection, he met two followers on the road to Emmaus, a town located about seven miles away from Jerusalem. The two had hoped that Jesus was the promised Messiah, but his death brought their dreams—and their faith—to a sudden end. And now there was a rumor going around that only added to their pain and confusion.

They said: "In addition, some of our women amazed us. They went to the tomb early this morning but didn't find his body. They came and told us that they had seen a vision of angels, who said he was alive. Then some of our companions went to the tomb and found it just as the women had said, but they did not see Jesus" (Luke 24:22–24).

The two were overcome with grief and disillusionment in light of the tragic events of the past few days. They had not yet made the connection between God's promises in Scripture and Jesus' death on the cross as part of God's plan to remove sin and restore our relationship with him. They were confused, doubting, and heartbroken.

Read Jesus' reaction: "He said to them, 'How foolish you are, and how slow to believe all that the prophets have spoken! Did not the Messiah have to suffer these things and then enter his glory?' And beginning with Moses and all the Prophets, he explained to them what was said in all the Scriptures concerning himself" (verses 25–27).

Looking back on their Emmaus road experience, the two disciples later realized that even before Jesus revealed himself plainly, they recognized him by the impact his words and the truth of Scripture had on their hearts (see verse 32).

The two followers were enthralled! Their doubts were lifted as Jesus opened the Scriptures to them, and they began to understand God's greater plan. Note that Jesus started at the beginning "with Moses" and continued with "all the Prophets." All of Scripture centers on Jesus, for it is the primary witness that Jesus is who he says he is.

## CONNECT [15 MINUTES]

Get the session started by discussing one or both of the following questions as a group:

- Briefly share your experience of the Lenten practice you did last week. The focus of this practice was to embrace the cross by letting go of something you needed to die to in order to receive new life. What did letting go of these things at the cross—like struggles or anxieties—require of you this week?

— or —

- What was the most helpful watchword you identified in your daily Scripture reading? How did God use it to challenge, encourage, or comfort you?

## DISCUSS [50 MINUTES]

For this week's study, you will spend extended time exploring the biblical foundation for our confidence that Jesus is the Messiah who saves us from sin.

1. It's human nature to seek to prove that the object of our trust is in fact trustworthy. We want to know that when someone makes a promise to us, we can rely on that person to keep it. This was true of the people in the Bible. We find that Abraham and Sarah, Moses, Gideon, and others all wanted to be sure they could trust God's promises. Listed below are Scripture passages that explore how each of these biblical characters wrestled with God's promises. Go around the group and have each person read aloud two or three verses at a time. Then use the questions that follow to continue your discussion.

   **Abraham and Sarah:** Read Genesis 17:15–22 and 18:10–15. What three words or phrases describe how Abraham responded to God's promises? How Sarah responded?

   **Moses:** Read Exodus 3:7–14. God promised Moses that he would rescue the Israelites from the Egyptians and that he would be with Moses when Moses spoke to Pharaoh. What stands out most to you about how Moses responded to God's promises?

   **Gideon:** Read Judges 6:11–18. Compare and contrast Gideon's response to God's promises with the responses of Abraham, Sarah, and Moses. How would you describe the similarities and differences? Based on each of these passages you've read, how would you characterize God's response when you have doubts about his promises?

2. The greatest promise God gave to his people is that he would send a Messiah to save them from sin. The Old Testament includes more than three hundred prophecies about this promised Savior who would come into the world and restore the relationship between God and humankind. What do the following verses say would happen to the Messiah?

**Psalm 41:9**

**Psalm 22:18**

**Psalm 22:1**

**Zechariah 12:10**

**Psalm 16:9–11**

3. The Gospels reveal that Jesus is the fulfillment of these prophecies. Again and again we read the words "so that Scripture would be fulfilled" in the context of Jesus' last days on earth. Jesus used his final days to offer us proof of who he is and why he came. How do the following verses show that Jesus fulfilled God's promises concerning the Messiah?

**His betrayal**—John 18:1–9

**His clothing**—John 19:23–24

**His being forsaken by God**—Matthew 27:46

**His side pierced**—John 19:34, 37

**His victory over death**—John 20:9

4. Read the full story of the two disciples who encountered the risen Jesus on the road to Emmaus in Luke 24:13–35. Consider how Jesus chose to interact with the two disciples in this story—when he shows up, what he says and does not say, and how his presence impacts them. Why do you think Jesus refrained from revealing who he was right away? What does his approach suggest about how he might choose to reveal himself to us today?

5. Looking back on their Emmaus road experience, the two disciples realized that even before Jesus revealed himself plainly, they recognized him by the impact his words and the truth of Scripture had on their hearts. How did this recognition impact their ability to have confidence in Christ—to trust his promises and to believe he was who he said he was? In what ways has the truth of Jesus' resurrection impacted your life recently?

## RESPOND [15 MINUTES]

Take a moment to reflect on what you've learned and experienced together in this study.

- How has reflecting on the proof the Scriptures provide about Jesus impacted your confidence in God's promises?

- Since you began this study, how has learning about the magnitude of Jesus' sacrifice on the cross changed the way you relate to Christ or understand who God is?

## PRAY [10 MINUTES]

Take a moment to give thanks for all the gifts that God provided at the cross. Ask him to remove any distractions that take your gaze away from Jesus' sacrifice. Record any prayer requests or praises so you and your group members can pray about them in the week ahead.

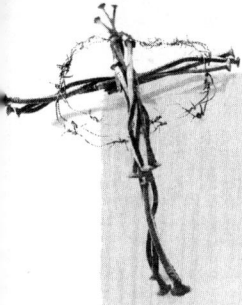

# LENTEN PRACTICE

*Let us then approach God's throne of grace with confidence, so that*
*we may receive mercy and find grace to help us in our time of need.*

HEBREWS 4:16

The story of Jesus' disciples from the Gospels to the book of Acts is one of contrasts. After Jesus' resurrection, he appeared to his followers for forty days. At one point, he instructed them to "go and make disciples of all nations, baptizing them in the name of the Father and of the Son and of the Holy Spirit, and teaching them to obey everything I have commanded you" (Matthew 28:19–20). Jesus gave them these final words before ascending into heaven:

> "You will receive power when the Holy Spirit comes on you; and you
> will be my witnesses in Jerusalem, and in all Judea and Samaria, and to
> the ends of the earth" (Acts 1:7–8).

The Gospels relate that on the night Jesus was arrested, all the disciples "deserted him and fled" (Mark 14:50). Peter even denied knowing Jesus three times (see Matthew 26:69–75). But as we move into the book of Acts, we find the disciples boldly proclaiming the gospel, answering Jesus' call to be his "witnesses" and to "make disciples of all nations." What prompted this profound change? What gave them this burst of confidence and enabled them to fulfill Jesus' Great Commission? They had received *power* from the Holy Spirit.

The invitation this week is to close out the season of Lent by thinking of who in your world needs to hear about Jesus' resurrection and receive the message of the gospel. Just as the disciples boldly shared their stories of faith and proclaimed the message of salvation to the nations, so you can confidently share your story of faith and proclaim the message of salvation to those in your world. Ask yourself, *Who is God placing on my heart to share about Christ?* Take some time to think about it and then lean into the confidence that you have been provided in Christ to go out and do it.

Here is a final overview of what each day will look like:

- Begin in the morning with a brief time of silence (one to two minutes). Then, in God's loving presence, reflect on these questions:

  ▸ *Who in my world needs to hear about Christ?*
  ▸ *What do I need to do (or am I doing) to reach out to that person?*

- Next, ask the Lord to speak to you through what you are about to read. Go over the Scripture passages for the morning slowly and prayerfully, paying attention to anything that sparks a connection between the text and your life. These are your **watchwords** for the day. They might be a promise, a word of wisdom, an admonition, a comfort, or an encouragement.

- Read your morning watchwords again, receiving what you read as God's words especially for you. Then reflect on the following questions:

  ▸ *What do I sense God is saying to me?*
  ▸ *If I took these words seriously, how would I respond?*

- Sometime later in the day, read the evening psalm slowly and prayerfully, again paying attention to any words, phrases, or verses that stand out to you. Write down your evening **watchwords** for this psalm.

- Read these watchwords again, and then reflect on the following questions:

  ▸ *What do I sense God is saying to me?*
  ▸ *If I took these words seriously, how would I respond?*

- Close by asking God to fill you with confidence to share the message of Christ. Invite him to use your watchwords to continue speaking to you throughout the rest of the day. Write down any other observations about your experience of reading God's Word and listening for his voice.

- At the end of the week, review your daily reflections and observations. What stands out most to you about what God is saying to you? Write your observations in the space provided or in your journal.

If you have been in a small group, consider sharing your observations from this week's practice with a friend or another member of the group one-on-one in the coming days.

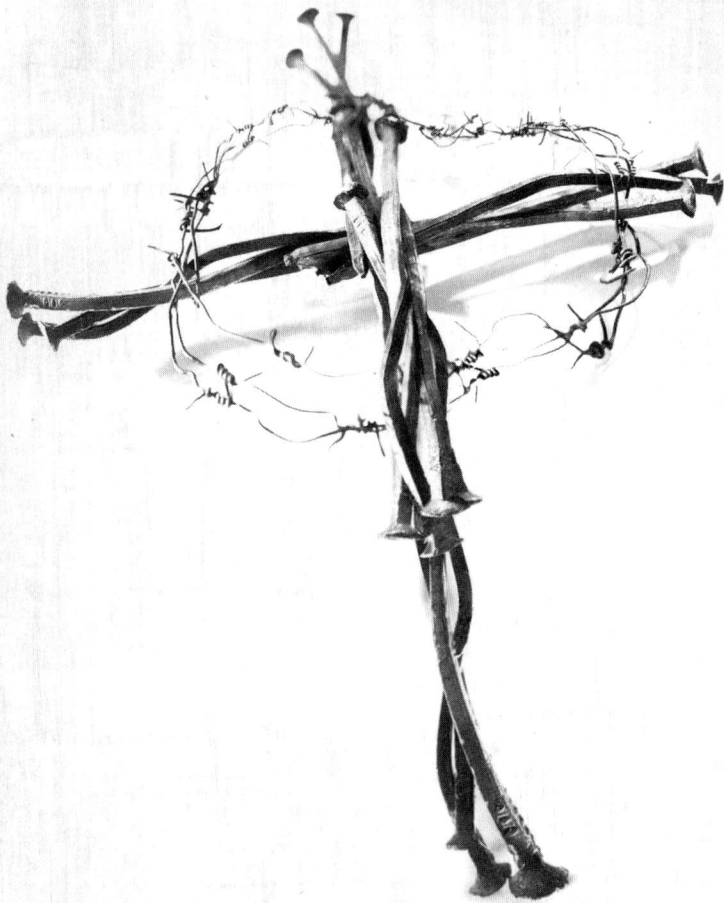

# DAY 36

## PREPARATION

Begin each day with a time of silence (one to two minutes). Be still for just a few moments to free your mind from distractions and worries so you can focus on your time with the Lord.

## REFLECTION

*Who in my world needs to hear about Christ? What do I need to do to reach out to that person?*

## MORNING READING

Remember each day to ask the Lord to speak to you through what you are about to read. Pay attention to any words, phrases, or verses that stand out to you.

- **Psalm:** Psalms 95; 105:1–11
- **Epistle:** Romans 15:5–13
- **Old Testament:** Exodus 12:1–11
- **Gospel:** John 3:16–21

**Watchwords** (anything that sparks a connection between the text and your life):

*What do I sense God is saying to me? If I took these words seriously, how would I respond?*

## EVENING READING

Once again, ask the Lord to speak to you through what you are about to read.

- **Psalm:** Psalm 106

**Watchwords:**

*What do I sense God is saying to me? If I took these words seriously, how would I respond?*

## CLOSE

Close by asking God to fill you with confidence to share the message of Christ. Journal any other observations about your experience of reading God's Word and listening for his voice.

# DAY 37

## REFLECTION

*Who in my world needs to hear about Christ? What am I doing to reach out to that person?*

## MORNING READING

- **Psalm:** Psalm 107:1–16
- **Epistle:** 2 Corinthians 6:1–18
- **Old Testament:** Exodus 12:12–20
- **Gospel:** Mark 15:40–47

**Watchwords:**

*What do I sense God is saying to me? If I took these words seriously, how would I respond?*

## EVENING READING

- **Psalm:** Psalm 108

**Watchwords:**

*What do I sense God is saying to me? If I took these words seriously, how would I respond?*

# DAY 38

## REFLECTION

*Who in my world needs to hear about Christ? What am I doing to reach out to that person?*

## MORNING READING

- **Psalm:** Psalm 110
- **Epistle:** 2 Corinthians 7:1–9
- **Old Testament:** Exodus 12:21–30
- **Gospel:** Mark 16:1–8

**Watchwords:**

*What do I sense God is saying to me? If I took these words seriously, how would I respond?*

## EVENING READING

- **Psalm:** Psalm 115

**Watchwords:**

*What do I sense God is saying to me? If I took these words seriously, how would I respond?*

# DAY 39

## REFLECTION

*Who in my world needs to hear about Christ? What am I doing to reach out to that person?*

## MORNING READING

- **Psalm:** Psalm 117
- **Epistle:** 2 Corinthians 7:10–16
- **Old Testament:** Exodus 12:31–42
- **Gospel:** Mark 16:9–14

**Watchwords:**

*What do I sense God is saying to me? If I took these words seriously, how would I respond?*

## EVENING READING

- **Psalm:** Psalm 118

**Watchwords:**

*What do I sense God is saying to me? If I took these words seriously, how would I respond?*

# Day 40

## REFLECTION

*Who in my world needs to hear about Christ? What am I doing to reach out to that person?*

## MORNING READING

- **Psalm:** Psalm 130
- **Epistle:** 2 Corinthians 8:1–15
- **Old Testament:** 1 Chronicles 16:23–30
- **Gospel:** Mark 16:15–20

**Watchwords:**

*What do I sense God is saying to me? If I took these words seriously, how would I respond?*

## EVENING READING

- **Psalm:** Psalm 16

**Watchwords:**

*What do I sense God is saying to me? If I took these words seriously, how would I respond?*

# WEEK IN REVIEW

Review the daily reflections and observations that you recorded during the course of this week. *What stands out most to you about what God is saying to you?*

Talk with your group about what study you may want to go through next. Put a date on the calendar for when you'll meet next to study God's Word and dive deeper into community.

# LEADER'S GUIDE

Thank you for your willingness to lead your group through this study! What you have chosen to do is valuable and will make a difference in the lives of others. *He Chose the Nails* is a five-session video study (with a bonus non-video session) built around video content and small-group interaction. As the group leader, imagine yourself as the host of a party. Your job is to take care of your guests by managing the details so that when your guests arrive, they can focus on one another and on the interaction around the topic for that session.

Your role as the group leader is not to answer all the questions or reteach the content—the video, book, and study guide will do most of that work. Your job is to guide the experience and cultivate your small group into a connected and engaged community. This will make it a place for members to process, question, and reflect—not necessarily to receive more instruction. There are several elements in this leader's guide that will help you as you structure your study and reflection time, so be sure to follow along and take advantage of each one.

## BEFORE YOU BEGIN

Before your first meeting, make sure the group members have a copy of this study guide. Alternately, you can hand out the study guides at your first meeting and give the members some time to look over the material and ask any preliminary questions. Also, make sure that the group members are aware they have access to the streaming videos at any time by following the instructions provided with this guide. During your first meeting, ask the members to provide their names, phone numbers, and email addresses so that you can keep in touch.

Generally, the ideal size for a group is eight to ten people, which will ensure that everyone has enough time to participate in discussions. If you have more people, break up the main group into smaller subgroups. Encourage those who show up at the first meeting to commit to attending the duration of the study, as this will help the group members get to know one another, create stability for the group, and help you know how best to prepare to lead the participants through the material.

Each session begins with an opening reflection. The questions that follow in the Connect section serve as icebreakers to get the group members thinking about the topic. In the rest of the study, it's generally not a good idea to have everyone answer every question—a free-flowing discussion is more desirable. But with the icebreaker question, you can go around the circle and ask each person to respond. Encourage shy people to share, but don't force them.

At your first meeting, let the members know that each session also contains daily Lenten practices for the week that will give them the opportunity to connect with God and prepare their hearts for Easter. Encourage them to do these practices by setting aside a brief amount of time in the morning and evening to talk with their heavenly Father. To get the most out of the practices, it is best if they don't rush them or leave them to the last minute to complete.

Let them know that, if they choose to do so, they can watch the video for the next session by accessing the streaming code provided with this study guide. Invite them to bring any questions and insights to your next meeting, especially if they had a breakthrough moment or didn't understand something.

## PREPARATION FOR EACH SESSION

As the leader, there are a few things you should do to best prepare for each meeting:

- **Read through the session.** This will help you become more familiar with the content and know how to structure the discussion times.

- **Decide how the videos will be used.** Determine whether you want the members to watch the videos ahead of time (again, via the streaming access code provided with this study guide) or together as a group.

- **Decide which questions you want to discuss.** Based on the length of your group discussions, you may not be able to get through all the questions. So look over the discussion questions provided in each session and mark which ones you definitely want to cover.

- **Be familiar with the questions you want to discuss.** When the group meets, you'll be watching the clock, so make sure you are familiar with the questions you have selected.

- **Pray for your group.** Pray for your group members and ask God to lead them as they study his Word and listen to his Spirit.

In many cases, there will be no one "right" answer to the questions. Answers will vary, especially when the group members are sharing their personal experiences.

## STRUCTURING THE DISCUSSION TIME

You will need to determine with your group how long you want your meetings to last so that you can plan your time accordingly. Suggested times for each section have been provided in this study guide, and if you adhere to these times, your group will meet for ninety minutes. However, many groups like to meet for two hours. If this describes your particular group, follow the times listed in the right-hand column of the chart below.

| SECTION | 90 Minutes | 120 Minutes |
|---|---|---|
| **CONNECT** (discuss one or more of the opening questions for the session) | 15 minutes | 20 minutes |
| **WATCH** (watch the teaching material together and take notes) | 20 minutes | 20 minutes |
| **DISCUSS** (discuss the study questions you selected ahead of time) | 35 minutes | 50 minutes |
| **RESPOND** (write down key takeaways) | 10 minutes | 15 minutes |
| **PRAY** (pray together and dismiss) | 10 minutes | 15 minutes |

For the bonus session, which does not have a Watch section, follow the times listed in the guide to meet for ninety minutes. Add five minutes to the Connect, Respond, and Pray sections and ten minutes to the Discuss section to meet for two hours.

Remember, as the group leader, it is up to you to keep track of the time and to keep things on schedule. You might want to set a timer for each segment so that both you and the group members know when the time is up. (There are some good phone apps for timers that play a gentle chime or other pleasant sound instead of a disruptive noise.)

Don't be concerned if group members are slow to share. People are often quiet when they are pulling together their ideas, and this might be a new experience for some of them. Just ask a question and let it hang in the air until someone shares. You can then say, "Thank you. What about others? What came to you when you watched that portion of the teaching?"

## GROUP DYNAMICS

Leading a group through *He Chose the Nails* will prove to be highly rewarding both to you and your group members. But you still may encounter challenges along the way! Discussions can get off track. Group members may not be sensitive to the needs and ideas of others. Some might worry that they will be expected to talk about matters that make them feel awkward. Others may express comments that result in disagreements.

To help ease this strain on you and the group, consider the following ground rules:

- When someone raises a question or comment that is off the main topic, suggest you deal with it another time, or, if you feel led to go in that direction, let the group know that you will be spending some time discussing it.

- If someone asks a question that you don't know how to answer, admit it and move on. At your discretion, feel free to invite group members to comment on questions that call for personal experience.

- If you find that one or two people are dominating the discussion time, direct a few questions to others in the group. Outside the main group time, ask the more dominating members to help you draw out the quieter ones. Work to make them part of the solution instead of part of the problem.

- When a disagreement occurs, encourage the group members to process the matter in love. Encourage those on opposite sides to restate what they heard the other side say about the matter, and then invite each side to evaluate if that perception is accurate. Lead the group in examining other passages related to the topic and look for common ground.

When any of these issues arise, encourage your group members to follow these words from Scripture: "Love one another" (John 13:34); "If it is possible, as far as it depends on you, live at peace with everyone" (Romans 12:18); "Whatever is true, whatever is noble, whatever is right, whatever is pure, whatever is lovely, whatever is admirable—if anything is excellent or praiseworthy—think about such things" (Philippians 4:8); and, "Everyone should be quick to listen, slow to speak and slow to become angry" (James 1:19). This will make your group time more rewarding and beneficial for everyone who attends.

Thank you for taking the time to lead your group. You are making a difference in your members' lives and having an impact on them as their prepare their hearts for Easter.

# NOTES

1. The season of Lent actually lasts for forty-six days, beginning on Ash Wednesday and ending at sundown on Holy Thursday. The forty days of fasting and penance exclude Sundays, which are considered feast days.

2. The "Daily Office" sounds like a workplace to the modern reader, but it comes from the Latin *officium divinum*, which means "divine duty." The *offices* refer to the morning and evening prayers.

3. Ann Voskamp, "A Holy Experience" blog, aholyexperience.com.

4. Cornelius Van Dam, "qr'," in *New International Dictionary of Old Testament Theology and Exegesis*, Willem A. VanGemeren, gen. ed., vol. 3 (Zondervan, 1997), 993.

5. J. A. Thompson and Elmer A. Martens, "šwb," in *New International Dictionary of Old Testament Theology and Exegesis*, Willem A. VanGemeren, gen. ed., vol. 4 (Zondervan, 1997), 56.

6. N. T. Wright, *Lent for Everyone: Matthew, Year A* (Westminster John Knox Press, 2011), 2.

7. Albert Haase, *Living the Lord's Prayer: The Way of the Disciple* (InterVarsity Press, 2009), 164.

8 Douglas Hill Jr., "A Nail Through Time: How This Tiny Tool Shaped Human History," Grayhill Woodworking LLC, https://www.grayhillwoodworkingllc.com/blog-3-1/a-nail-through-time-how-this-tiny-tool-shaped-human-history?srsltid=AfmBOoqfAiJvYOPYG eEJP4AcsTupOvPXMunZnfStqvnIV7wSlqUkOdX9.

9. Hans Bietenhard, "Enemy, Enmity, Hate," in *New International Dictionary of New Testament Theology*, Colin Brown, gen. ed., vol. 1 (Zondervan, 1975, 1986), 553.

10. "All of this is a gift from God, who brought us back to himself through Christ. . . . For God was in Christ, reconciling the world to himself" (2 Corinthians 5:18–19 NLT).

11. Timothy J. Keller, "More Wicked but More Loved," February 4, 2015, dailykeller.com.

12. Charles Spurgeon, "Our Lord's Entrance Within the Veil," from a sermon preached on March 17, 1889, https://www.spurgeon.org/resource-library/sermons/our-lords-entrance-within-the-veil/#flipbook/.

13. "A symbol of God's unapproachability, this curtain was made of blue, purple, scarlet, and fine twisted linen embroidered with figures of cherubim (Exodus 26:31–37; 36:35). It was hung with golden hooks upon four pillars of acacia wood overlaid with gold which were set in sockets or bases of silver. It is likely that the curtain was quite thick to correspond with its great size." "Curtain," in *Zondervan Illustrated Bible Dictionary*, ed. J. D. Douglas and Merrill C. Tenney, revised by Moisés Silva (Zondervan, 1987, 2011), 323.

14. Eugene H. Peterson, *Tell It Slant: A Conversation on the Language of Jesus in His Stories and Prayers* (Wm. B. Eerdmans, 2008), 269.
15. A. W. Tozer, *The Pursuit of God* (CreateSpace Independent Publishing, 2014), 23.
16. A. W. Tozer, *Tozer on the Almighty God: A 365-Day Devotional* (Moody Publishers, 2004).
17. Eugene H. Peterson, *The Jesus Way: A Conversation on the Ways that Jesus Is the Way* (Wm. B. Eerdmans, 2007), 22.
18  Kaufmann Kohler and Emil G. Hirsch, "Crucifixion," Jew Encyclopedia, https://jewish encyclopedia.com/articles/4782-crucifixion.
19. Paraphrase of W. Harold Mare, "1 Corinthians," in *The Expositor's Bible Commentary*, Frank E. Gaebelein, gen. ed., vol. 10 (Zondervan, 1976), 223.
20. John Ortberg, *Soul Keeping: Caring for the Most Important Part of You* (Zondervan, 2014), 122.
21. Dallas Willard, *Renovation of the Heart: Putting On the Character of Christ* (NavPress, 2002), 227.
22. Dallas Willard, "A Conversation on Pain and Suffering," November 19–20, 2011, https://dwillard.org/resources/audio/pain-and-suffering.
23. Eugene H. Peterson, *A Long Obedience in the Same Direction: Discipleship in an Instant Society* (InterVarsity Press, 1980, 2000), 100.
24. Max Lucado, *He Chose the Nails: What God Did to Win Your Heart* (Thomas Nelson, 2000), 139–140.
25. Lucado, *He Chose the Nails*, 140.
26. A. W. Tozer, *The Pursuit of God* (Christian Publications, Inc., 1948).

# About Max Lucado

Photography by Amanda Mae Steele

Since entering the ministry in 1978, Max Lucado has served churches in Miami, Florida; Rio de Janeiro, Brazil; and San Antonio, Texas. He currently serves as the teaching minister of Oak Hills Church in San Antonio. He is the recipient of the 2021 ECPA Pinnacle Award for his outstanding contribution to the publishing industry and society at large. He is America's bestselling inspirational author with more than 150 million products in print. Visit his website at MaxLucado.com.

**Join the Max Lucado Community:**
Facebook.com/MaxLucado
Instagram.com/MaxLucado
X.com/MaxLucado
YouTube.com/MaxLucadoOfficial